Fighting Dragons in Heels!

Creativity through Divorce

By:

Sarah Vaden Codner

Vadeninc.com

Since the writing of this book, Vaden Inc. has continued to help moms. Please be our guest and visit **vadeninc.com** *for continued support and encouragement. Be sure to sign up for newsletters, read blogs, and obtain free gifts. As well, a workbook has been created to further help you, which can also be found on the website.*

I look forward to serving you.

Dedicated to:

Those who will learn to believe in themselves.

Vaden

❧VADEN INC.❧

4

Acknowledgements

Special thanks to my son; he helped me create the book cover. I will cherish the time we took to put it together. Every smirk you gave as I tried to draw and every idea you gave, I have locked in my memory. I thank you for not just the help with the cover, but for making me a better person.

Special thanks to my daughter; she gave me permission to use her stuffed animal story to help reach other moms. Her stuffed animal "Boo" has been many a mile with us. Also, I want to thank her for her spontaneity in every situation and exuberance for life. You too, make me a better person.

You two are my heart.

Contents

Forward……………………….…………chapter 1

Introduction……………………………..chapter 2

Recycle, Reclaim and Rebuild…………..…chapter 3

Turn the Page……………………………chapter 4

Mind Tricks…………….…….…………chapter 5

Grief/Anger……………….……………..chapter 6

Me Me Me…………………………….....chapter 7

Quotes……………………………….....chapter 8

Money…………………….……………chapter 9

Conclusion……………….……………chapter 10

VADEN INC.

8

Chapter 1

Forward

My heart goes out to those who are in imminent danger of divorce. There really are no words to describe the aching of your body, mind and spirit. I have heard it described as if a tsunami rushes over the land of your life. You are sucked out to the ocean of despair. It feels useless to get up because waves continue to crash upon your desolate land and drag you out into the depths of the waters. There is no air to breath and you feel as if you have delirium. And maybe you do for a time because you are unable to make sound decisions or even understand what is happening to your world. All you know is the constant pounding of waves and your lungs drawing in more of the deep sea.

I too felt this unyielding asphyxiation of the ocean. I had that feeling in the pit of my stomach. I sensed impending doom. It sounds so dramatic to put it in words. But, it was traumatic. Once you have experienced it, you will forever be changed. I can remember one night in particular that touched me all the way to my soul. However, it was a pivotal night that would change my life.

One night in the middle of the night I saw red. By this point, my husband was sleeping on the sofa, he gave excuses such as falling asleep watching T.V., and he was too hot in the bedroom and on and on it would go. Well, that particular night I awoke alone in bed and too hot. This is odd, because I am never too hot. I was so uncomfortable I actually got out of bed to change the thermostat. I went back to my room

and tried to sleep. I tossed and turned. I could not sleep. Again, I became so hot I had to get out of bed. I stood by the side of the bed for a moment trying to think of what I should do next. I had already turned the air down once. But for some reason, I was compelled to go turn it down again. As I walked by my husband, asleep on the sofa, his cell phone lit up, no sound. I ignored it and went and turned the thermostat down even more. I walked back by the sofa and it crossed my mind that his phone must be on silent and what if someone was injured or needed help of some sort. I picked up the phone and looked at it. It was a text message that had an asterisk on it. I thought to myself, it must be a mistake. I went back to bed. But then I immediately shot up out of bed and grabbed his cell phone and something inside of me, had me reply an asterisk. Immediately a response, it said, "Are you awake? I love you"... WHAT? Who was sending my husband this message in the middle of the night? I looked to see the number. I did not recognize it, so I started to try and match it with names I had suspected in the past. None of them matched the numbers of women I suspected; I was beginning to feel a little silly and guilty for my thoughts. But the message was there in black and white to see. I then started at the top of his phone list and opening up every female name to see if I could find a matching number. When I came to a particular name, the number matched. I had never before heard of this person's name. I flipped on every light in the living room, threw the phone at my husband and yelled "Who the HELL is_____?" He woke with a start. He could hardly talk. He tried to deny it stuttering and stammering every time he tried to speak, he tried to talk his way out of the message and then when I dialed the number back he turned the situation trying to say I was stirring up trouble. He could not even make it through the conversation without getting up and getting some water. His throat kept getting so dry. He finally told me it was one

of the individuals I had suspected; he just had her under a different name in his phone. I asked if that was not a bit deceitful. I demanded why he was still talking with her. I had asked him to stop all communication. His reply was, "I didn't know you meant texting too". I screamed at this point, "I meant texting, talking or even smoke signals!" And that was the end for me. I was done.

I have found this memory to be the hardest to write, edit, and re-read. I get short of breath, my palms get sweaty and my stomach burns. I could have told of many other scenarios, but this one seems so critical to share. I want you as the reader to know; I felt every one of those waves. I experienced the lack of oxygen. I came face to face with my emotional torment.

This book is about recovering from your traumatic events. You may have to take it in bite size pieces. But, I can remember, craving for something to hold onto as I bounced around on the tossing seas. Use this book as your safety net, as your lifesaver. If the waves are still coming in too strong, start with chapter 8 about quotes. Keep in mind, the waves still come in, but now, I can stand as they lap at my feet.

VADEN INC.

Empty advice or profound pontification has no place when one is in the throws of divorce. Paul Simon and Garfunkel proclaimed in their song there were fifty ways to leave your lover.

"Just slip out the back, Jack
make a new plan, Stan
don't need to be coy, Roy"…
"hop on the bus, Gus
just drop off the key, Lee
and get yourself free."

Theses ideas are simple and attainable. Divorcees can be resilient. They just need to be given proper tools. They need access to survival skills.

Some may argue divorce rates are declining in the United States. Research from the 2009 U.S. Census Bureau, reveals each states divorce rate for the past twelve months. A snap shot from coast to coast reveals divorce is still prevalent.

The divorce rate for women in New York City is 7.3/1,000 households. The divorce rate for women In Oklahoma City skyrockets at 14.1/1,000 households. The divorce rate in California surpasses New York at 8.9/1,000 households. That being said, the divorce rate is still not zero. Divorces continue. Marriages continue to fall apart.

To help those traveling this course is vital to our countries' future. If we can empower a single woman or single mom to have the confidence to better herself, think of the impact that the woman will have on not just her own life, but her children, her friends, her co-workers, society as a whole.

Single Moms comprise 29% of American households. This is according to the U.S. Census. Numerous websites reveal undesirable statistics for children of single mothers.

-Children are more likely to drop out of school
-Children are more likely to use drugs and or have other addictions
-Children are more likely to have behavioral or psychiatric problems
-Children are more likely to fail at their own relationships
-Children are more likely to raise their own children out of wedlock
-Children are more likely to live in or be unable to get out of poverty
-Children are more likely to have a higher incident of suicide
-Children are more likely to become homeless or be runaways

However, there is also positive research. A new examination of single moms suggests ways to eliminate or at least reduce the above risks. Minimizing the weakness of being a single mom and building on the strengths is at the core of reversing these negative outcomes.

Single moms need to be given stability and security to be able to provide consistent love. Think about this quote from Bill Richardson.

"Raising a family is difficult enough. But it's even more difficult for single parents struggling to make ends meet. They don't' need more obstacles. They need more opportunities."

Single moms can provide daily family rituals like having dinner, cuddle time, and imposing limits and boundaries for their children. Single moms have the upper hand without having another spouse to have to negotiate problems or situations. As well, single moms have the ability to have a special bond with their children because they are likely to spend time with their children reading and talking with them. As well, a working single mom is a great role model of strength and endurance.

Because of this research, single mom conferences are being scheduled all over the country. Remember the Chinese proverb. "Give a man a fish and you feed him for a day. Teach a man to fish and you feed him for a lifetime." I expect the same is true of a woman, but she then educates a family and therefore educates our countries future.

Memories, properties, personal items, children and more are all a part in the untying the knots of a marriage. As hurtful and painful as it is when each knot loosens, there is life after divorce. Everyone is able to find his or her way, but sometimes it is nice to get a little advice from someone who's been there. The unwinding of one life leads to the weaving of a different life.

Divorce has set the stage for me to see not only myself but also others up close and personal. I have seen many scared people and felt myself the wounds of divorce. I have seen both men and women struggle through their divorces. It has been grossly fascinating to see some wilt and loose the ability to re-awaken their lives. And yet others, still injured, battered and bruised, carry on and find a force within them to better themselves.

This book is about making the choice to become a force to be reckoned with. My divorce was hard. I will forever be changed. As strange as it sounds, I have become thankful for the choices my ex-husband made, so I could have the life I have created now. You will not find the pages of this book filled with negativity or ex-husband bashing. I did not get a divorce because things were going great. However, he remains the father of my children and deserves all the respect that comes with that position.

Any memoires that are told are from my recollection. I intentionally did not go into great details so as to protect those involved. Any accounts that are given are intended for the sole purpose of the readers understanding. As well, the entire book is for the greater good for women to have optimism, support and encouragement from their individual divorces. Sometimes, a woman needs to know another woman's story. This allows her to know the author not only can have sympathy but empathy. This leads to growth, which in turn leads to the better good of mankind.

Divorce is happening. I have a passion to help others take hold of their own lives and believe in themselves. I currently live in a state where the divorce rate is second highest in the Nation. I had to find the courage to share a piece of my life to help others. There are law books, technical books and psychological books about divorce. But, I wanted to grasp the feelings that one goes through in divorce and provide one with a desire to persevere. Simple strategies and attainable goals are at the fingertips of the reader. This book offers common sense. It gives concrete ideas to act upon to start life now, today. I think "Fighting Dragons in heels!" is a refreshing resource for divorcees. I hope you truly fall head over *heels* for it.

Vaden

Chapter 2

INTRODUCTION

Welcome to divorce. Life as you once knew it just got rocked to its core. Divorce has been described as a death, but worse, because the other person doesn't die. It's intolerable. The person who was supposed to love, honor, and cherish you, just betrayed you, your children, your family, your hopes and dreams. But you have to keep on dealing with those things. Death is final, betrayal is bitter. Divorce is a journey no one should have to travel, but unfortunately, it is the reality of our world. I've been there, your best friend has been there, your daughter has been there, someone you know has been there, or you are there now. You need some survival skills. Divorce can damage you for a lifetime or you can accept the adventure and create something better.

Abandoned, deceived, cheated on, or even treated with cruelty, that is divorce. I have been divorced. My entire world has been shaken. My life has crumbled to its foundation. But, I refused to give up or give in, for seven years now. I continued this journey of life and propelled myself into my future. I used the ideas in this book during my divorce and even used many during my father's death. I have found a way to deal with life's changes.

As well, my friends have used these strategies and begged me for more. The expectation is for you to learn methods to

take control of your own life. My hope is that you will end up having fun with these survival skills and conquer any heartache, break-up, challenge, difficulty, or change that you encounter.

Coping skills are the key to survival. If you've lived long enough, you know life is hard. You have a mechanism for dealing with stress. Now, whether that mechanism is protective, productive, beneficial or destructive, is the key. I was unaware so many others had no idea of how to deal with bad situations or circumstances. It just so happens that my qualities and strengths are my secret weapons against adversity. My life has fine-tuned these characteristics.

When I was a little girl I longed to be old enough to be a cheerleader. The day finally came for tryouts. I was so excited. I could hardly wait to learn all the cheers, learn to climb to the top of the pyramids and put on those cute little pleated skirts. I knew I was going to pull my long brown hair up into a ponytail and put a great big white bow in it. Only problem was, I did not make the team. I couldn't believe it. I didn't understand why, I had wanted it so badly, hadn't that been enough??? I cried, I cried hard that night after try-outs. My entire family knew how upset I was. My father even brought home a beautiful violet plant to cheer me up.

Then and there that night, my secret weapon against hardships was born. After I stopped crying, I started asking myself questions. How was I different from the girls who had been chosen for the cheerleading squad? I came up with a couple of ideas such as I was unable to do a complete split and my jumps were only mediocre. Then I thought maybe there were things that I didn't even know about cheerleading, because I had never been a cheerleader. So, that night I put in motion a plan to become a cheerleader by

the next year. I bought a book about cheerleading and read as much as I could. I sought out an older successful friend who was a cheerleader for advice. I stretched everyday until I could do a split, and I wore ankle weights to strengthen my legs for higher jumps. It *was* the eighties after all! I proudly made the squad every year after that! I have learned through my life experiences that some of my best characteristics are resilience and persistence.

No matter how many times I get knocked down, I keep getting up again. I just keep banging my head against that wall; I think, either the wall is going to give or my head is going to break. To be honest, these qualities annoy the tar out of me. They may be my best qualities, but on the flip side, they are the most aggravating. Sometimes, I wish I could say that's it, that's the end of my rope, no more for me, thank you. But no, somehow, some way, this persistence strikes me every time. I give it one more try. That may sound odd, but I know on my darkest days with time, that little voice of hope pops up, and I'm ready to attack my problems from another angle.

Luckily for me, along with persistence, I have been given the valuable qualities of creativity and imagination. I refuse to be trapped inside a box. I believe in, "if there is a will, there is a way." So my mind is constantly thinking of new ways to address a problem or situation. I know I will lean on these strengths of persistence and creativity to fight my battles.

Identifying just these qualities, I know I already have an attack plan for anything that comes my way. I assumed my friends had been laughing at my crazy antics, when in fact they were amazed at my coping skills. All of this led me to start writing down my "tricks of the trade." I, too, was astonished at how many types of skills I had within me. After

much persuasion from my friends, family and even my lawyers, I decided to share. I did not enjoy my struggles, who does? But, maybe I can share and help you through yours, like I have helped so many of my friends and myself. So, consider yourself my friend as hopefully we can work through your difficulties.

Divorce can lead you to a place where you don't even recognize yourself. As if that's not the worst, you don't know where to begin to change yourself or your circumstances. There is hope. There are concrete strategies that can be learned. All you have to do is take the action to try. You can either stay emotionally, physically, or even spiritually trapped where you are, or you can choose to change. The choice is yours.

Putting closure on your past is difficult and emotionally painful. I say, let's hit it right on, deal with it, and move out of that phase. I think this is a particularly hard time, because you have to face the truth. Bluntly, I was in denial about my marriage. Prior to my divorce, I had been too busy trying to keep everything together. And above all that, keep the appearance that everything was just fine and dandy. It was exhausting to say the least. I was in such denial. Looking back on it now, I realize I saw things with my own two eyes that no wife should ever have to see, let alone tolerate or go through. But still, I can remember trying to defend my marriage in my lawyer's office. She finally very directly said…"Your problem has been that you *both* loved him." I felt like I had been jolted out of a sound sleep. This was my first step to truth. Once the truth had been presented, I was able to begin to make sound judgments and decisions about the situation. I was no longer ruled by confusion or emotion.

Facing your past frees you emotionally. Whether you made mistakes, or if someone else did you wrong, you can see it objectively. Now, here comes the choice. One can get stuck at this point, so be careful. Once you see the truth, you can choose to keep thinking about what you shoulda, coulda, woulda done, or accept it as part of your past and move on. This is the part that builds character. If you can change your own bad ways, you have become a better person. If you can see where another person hurt you, and you can learn how to prevent that from happening next time, you have become a better person. I don't mean you are no longer affected by someone else's actions. However, the key is your reaction to them. If their actions kill your spirit, they have won. Your divorce is soon to be an event in your past.

My mother and I have always described life-changing events such as graduations, marriages, new jobs, births or even deaths, as "new threads in our tapestry of life." These events bring joy and hardship alike. Up close, each event is personal, emotional and daily consuming. But they only make up a single moment of your life. Your life is made up of many moments or in this case many "threads." You can only see the design or picture of your life/tapestry when you step back to admire or critique. Remember you are much more and have much more to do in your life. You are bigger than this moment.

Early in my separation I had wise counsel. I had gone to see a very special friend. I tried to tell her how horrible my marriage had been and specific things that had happened, on and on I went. What a blessing this person would not let me wallow in my sorrows! I am going to tell you exactly what she said, because it helped me and I hope it will help you. She cut me off and said, "Wait a minute. No one close

to you or even remotely close to you thinks you should stay in this marriage. That being said, you have your entire future with which to look forward. I want you to think of what you want to do and who you want to be. And while you are at it, dream big because you are that important to your children, your family, and society as a whole." I hope you have someone in your life that can be that direct and honest with you. If you don't, there it is; it's that simple. I could keep complaining about how wrong I had been done. Or, I could dream again. I chose to dream. You also get a second chance. It is like getting a "redo" in life. You see, the divorce itself is just the beginning.

When you truly realize that your divorce only represents a moment in time, your view of the world changes. And, as I accept my past, I admit there was a time I gladly revolved around my ex-husband and his priorities. But then I stepped into reality. I got a divorce, because in my situation it was the right thing to do. But even if it's the right choice, it does not mean it is not difficult. Divorce takes a toll on a person. Scars are inevitable when you walk away from a marriage. However, the idea is not that divorce is the *finished* product. Instead, it is the end of one thing and the beginning of another.

I continued to have "poor me" moments. But, I made the decision that only those very close to me would know my true inner struggles. I chose to show the side of me to the world of a strong and determined woman. I had many resources at my fingertips including my education, background, the support of two loving parents and friends. As my new life began to unfold, I found strength and inner peace. My life turned around when I realized I had to follow what I truly believed. I had to hold fast to my core beliefs. I

no longer was bound to my old life and was able to forget and forgive those in my past as well as myself.

I found hope and a truer way of life. Integrity, though not always fun or easy, was the reward. I now live in reality. I remember those first days when I was going through my divorce. I felt I had been told so many lies by so many. I could not differentiate between what was real and what was not. I remember walking around my new town house, reaching out and touching the walls. I wanted to make sure even the walls were real. I wanted to know for sure what would stand the test of time versus what would crumble. I wanted to feel safe again. Slowly, I was able to regain a sense of security. It took months of sorting through conversations and reminiscing about things that had taken place. I was afraid to do this at first. I was afraid I might find I had not been loved. The reality was just that. But, by the time I came to that realization, I better understood both my ex-husband's personality as well as my own. The rest of the reality was I might not have been loved. But I had so much more love from my family members and friends to make up for any inadequacy. And who doesn't have inadequacies? I knew I had loved him and given him all I knew how to and had been willing to learn more and give more. However, I also learned I could never love him enough for the both of us.

Divorce is the destruction of an idea, an idea that you put your faith into and which disappointed you. So how does one even begin to start the healing process of a destroyed marriage? The answer to healing is part time and part choice. Time just happens. For the other part, you must accept your past and find your future. Focus your thoughts and actions on potential opportunities. The devil (if you believe) wants you to think you have been defeated and that

life is impossible. I am proof that my old life pales in comparison to my life now. Actually, my past was not a life; it was a slow suffocation of my spirit and something that drove me into a situational depression. Interestingly, I never had depression until I met my ex-husband. Since my divorce, I continue to have the usual trials of life. I have even endured the sudden death of my father. None of these difficult times have thrown me into depression. My lawyers marveled at how well I handled my divorce. I would just laugh and say I had a husband-ectomy (which in medical terms means a removal of/or something cut out), and I was no longer depressed. Once you make the choice to focus on your future, the fun comes into play. You may think some of these ideas are a little off the wall. You may be right, but I dare say you will enjoy yourself.

There are two phrases you need to add to your repertoire of speech. You need to arm yourself and, better yet, your best friends and family with these words. They will be your mantra and your motivation. When all looks glum and dismal these sayings will put a smile on your face and get you moving again. It will be fun for you to find new ways to use and abuse these phrases. The first phrase speaks for itself and needs no explanation. It is multi-generational and multi-motivational. It is "put your big girl panties on!" I don't know about you, but I used to love Wonder Woman Underoos. I never had a pair, but my best friend did when we were four years old. Needless to say, I am past this practice now, but…my best friend used to let me wear her Wonder Woman Underoos. I loved those panties and matching undershirt. The image of me in those Underoos always comes to mind when I say or hear "put your big girl panties on." Now, if I could have a gold lasso and an invisible jet, I could really rock this world.

I say the phrase is multi-generational, because I used it on my mother one night. I had invited her to ride with me to church that evening. At the time, she had been having terrible knee problems and found it difficult to drive for extended periods of time. However, in a moment of single mom dementia (an ailment I am sure I share with hundreds), I forgot to pick her up and did not realize until I was at the door of the church and she called me on my cell phone. There was no point in coming up with an excuse. I had just flat out forgotten. I apologized and then told her to "put her big girl panties on" and come on to church. When she arrived, she looked rather smug. She came right up to me and said "Well, I've got 'em on!" I asked forgetting what I had said earlier "got what on?" She replied, "I did just what you said, I put my big girl panties on and drove myself here." Let that be a lesson to all of us. If my, at the time seventy-two-year-old mother can put her big girl panties on, there is power in those panties.

The other phrase needs a little explaining. Once you have been around me for a little bit, it takes no time to figure out that I love shoes. I always have loved shoes, probably always will, and the higher the heel the better. It is well known family knowledge that when I was two years old I was already gracefully wearing high heels. My mother tells of dinner parties she and my father would have. She says after dinner the adults would be sitting around the table and the ladies would slide their shoes off to relax. Apparently, I would go and snag them and be found later wearing them.

Also, I remember going every Thanksgiving as a child to buy a new pair of plastic (toy) high heels. I would dance to the Macy's day parade on TV. That was until the shoes would break. For some reason the plastic would never withstand my rocket kicks.

As a grown woman my passion for shoes has continued. I admit, to this day I fall in love with shoes. If a pair catches my eye, it is hard to resist. Once, I found a pair of sandals that cost well over five hundred dollars. I walked away…and then turned around and went right back to them. During the entire turn about I was trying to justify the cost. This walk about rotation happened four times. I am sure the salesclerk found this quite amusing. I finally was able to break the spell when I realized the cost for the sandals was more than my monthly car payment at the time. All of this said, my friends know I love shoes. I am the one friends ask if the shoe looks good and what outfit would work best with it. I am known for coordinating my outfit around my shoes instead of the other way around. On a trip, I always manage to take more shoes then there are days in my vacation. I am known as the shoe guru.

That leads us to how our next phrase came into existence. One of my friends bought a pair of black high heels (my specialty), and she wondered if they were keepers. She brought them to me for final inspection and thoughts. I thought they were wonderful. They had the best heel height to make her leg look longer; they had straps in all the right places to make her calves look smaller. Right on the top of the toes sat a black patent flower. They were splendid shoes, classic with a touch of flare. She drove home with her prize shoes. However, a little bit later she called distraught over something she had found out she had to do the next day. After we discussed her situation thoroughly, I finally told her the only way to get through it was to put her new shoes on and "put one flower foot in front of the other." And thus was born our new power phrase, "just put one flower foot in front of the other and get it done." You will be

amazed how well these phrases fit into your life as well. I hope they bring you smiles and miles of motivation.

There is one more key phrase I would like you to keep saying to yourself. There will be days you won't feel like saying it, say it anyway. There will be days you will not even resemble the phrase, but I want you to say it anyway. There will be days you will hardly have the strength to utter the words, say it anyway. And the phrase is..."You ain't seen nothin' yet!" There has been many a night, I confess, I have been too tired to change out of my clothes into pajamas. To bed I went; fully clothed with make-up, and hair in place. I did manage to walk out of my shoes. As my head would hit the pillow, with a smirk on my face, I would manage to utter, "You ain't seen nothin' yet!" To be honest, I did not want to see what I looked like the next morning. Inevitably, I would have mascara on my pillow, lipstick across the back of my hand, and hair going every direction. I would just put myself back together and out the door I would go with my mantra on my mind..."You ain't seen nothin' yet!" Sometimes you just gotta be your own cheerleader.

This book is intended to re-energize and re-focus you on your abilities. No one is spared from problems in this world. You may have noticed it seems that some have life a little bit easier than others. But, if you are honest you will also notice there are always those around you who have struggles. Your perspective on your own problems is the key. My lawyers sat in astonishment and disgust at our first meetings when I re-counted my married life for the past ten years. As the divorce proceeded and more and more was unveiled, my lawyers were amazed at my resilience. My attorneys told me I had a gift and should share it. At that time in my life, sharing was too painful. Now, I tell people I am happily divorced and am the happiest I have ever been. I continue

VADEN INC.

to have bad things happen to me. I have good and bad days just like everyone else, because I choose to live life. When you decide to be a part of the world, it keeps happening around you, too.

However, I have armed myself with coping skills that push me forward, not back. I am now able to write this book without resentment or anger towards my ex-husband, his family or his lawyer. I thank them for being who they are and doing the things they did. It allowed me to get out of their life and grow to be the strong woman I am today, someone constantly living in reality. And although my struggles may be different from yours, the same feelings still emerge. I want you to learn you are in control of your emotions and know the feeling that control gives you in your life. So, put your big girl panties on and put one flower foot in front of the other. We have a journey to start so you can begin your new life. It is waiting for you. You just have to have the courage to take it.

It's about making a choice. The reality was I had to go out and make a living during the day, and I had to come home and be a loving mother. My mother once said I was going to have to learn to fight dragons during the day and then come home to the safety of my cave. I decided to fight dragons in heels.

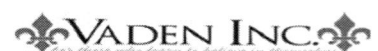

Chapter 3

RECYLCE, RECLAIM AND REBUILD BUT DON'T MESS WITH "BOO"!!

He was a pale shade of yellow with fabric more lustrous than velvet. His face was shaped like a bear with two rounded ears, an upside down pale pink triangle for a nose, and slender golden thread outlined his up-turned mouth. He lay in wait in the nursery for her to come. Upon her arrival and passage of milestones, she affectionately named him "Boo." He is not a human member of our family, but that little stuffed animal holds a place of honor and respect. He has smothered tears, stomped out anger and provided strength in times of fear. Boo, now the color of gray (even when washed in Clorox®), satin piping hanging from his edges, tattered seams and worn out fabric, still is the key to tranquility in our household. We go nowhere and do nothing without Boo. Boo has become part of my to-do lists. As I go out the door, I grab my cell phone, grab my purse, grab my keys, and as I lock the door, I turn to see that Boo is safely in my daughter's arms. As we get ready for bed, we check to see if we have accomplished baths, brushed hair and teeth, put clothes out for the next day, pajamas on and…where is Boo?

Boo has clout. As my little girl grows older, calming her has often been as simple as finding Boo. Just the mention of his name can begin to ease her troubles. As a matter of fact, the original Boo has been lost, and he has now been replaced twice. The surrogates have weathered just fine, because the power was in the name.

We put great emphasis on things we name. We have books upon books with baby names. We try different names on to see how they fit. We make sure they sound good with our last name. We verify that initials are not bad abbreviations. I remember going through the process of picking out baby names. My main goal was for my children to have what I thought were dignified names. I did not want them to have a name that other children would make fun of or use to make funny rhymes.

I remember some friends whose last name was "Line." One evening we all laughed hysterically thinking of names for them to give their future children. "Cruise Line," "Panty Line," "Dotted Line." "Under Line," "State Line." We got a bit silly that night. The couple did eventually have children. They did not use any of the names we had come up with that night. They, too, went the more dignified route.

Names have meaning. They identify us and distinguish us from others. Even nicknames display a sense of sentiment. Think about these nicknames, "Doc, Maverick, Braveheart, Lips, Barracuda, or even Diva." We trademark, copyright and brand items throughout our lives. A trademark blog posted in October 11, 2002, revealed that in Hong Kong in 1874, there was a registered trademark for NESTLES EAGLE BRAND™ condensed milk. Apparently, it is still in use today, and Borden's in the US owns EAGLE BRAND™ condensed milk. On this same site, I found it interesting that

"Brett Doyle argued that S.P.Q.R. should be deemed to be a mark for municipal services in use for two millennia." S.P.Q.R. stands for Senatus Populusque Romanus. It was used as a signature of sorts for the Roman government. They would stamp it on coins and buildings and fountains and manhole covers. This was done for the public to see. And yet another online site "WikiAnswers" explained the "oldest food trademark still in use in the US has been on cans of Underwood's Deviled Ham™ since 1866."

All of these finds fascinate me. I love to make a rich chocolate pie with condensed milk, I have always been interested in Roman history, and I cannot tell you how many stuffed green peppers I have eaten that my grandmother made with Underwood's Deviled Ham™. The bottom line is that names are important and influential throughout time and cultures.

Ancient Greeks and Greeks today celebrate "Name Day." This day commemorates you if you were named after one of the saints. On that day people bring small gifts and the hostess of the house makes sweets and hors d'oeuvres. "Name Day" is considered more important than one's birthday. Along those same lines the ancient Greeks used to think the spoken word was powerful. So, just saying something out loud can give the object life and authority.

To expand our minds, we must take what we learned from yesterday, educate ourselves today and repackage the knowledge from yesterday and today to create a new way of life. Train your brain to create positive surroundings. Try to find the good in every situation. This is not easy, it takes effort and creativity. I am not saying you have to be happy when bad things happen to you. Hurtful events do feel terrible. And no one likes going through them. However, we

can grow, learn, or even change if we want. We can also stop growing, refuse to learn and refuse to move forward with our lives. Again, I choose to live and be hurt again, rather than stand still and inevitably am hurt again anyway. I am not happy with status quo. I like figuring out new ways to progress. But for our open wounds to heal, we need a formula. I found a way to recycle and reuse good things and rename and repackage bad things to my advantage.

With all this in mind…I re-named my ex-husband. I never refer to him by his given name. All my acquaintances, fellow employees, friends and family members also refer to him by his "new" name. He is even in my cell phone under this new name. And now, I have to think about what his actual name is when I am talking to him.

I read that narcissists loved to hear the sound of their own name. This only fueled my enthusiasm for my new found re-name game. One of my friends and I started amusing ourselves whenever we happened to see my ex-husband. She would greet him with a friendly hello and address him with a name that started with the first letter of his real name. So, for example had his name been Robert, she would have called him Ronald or Regan or Rupert or, the name was different every time. He tried to correct her at first. She would smile innocently and apologize. But the very next time she would be ready with yet another name. Eventually, he stopped trying to rectify the situation. I would be so amused it would help me from crying.

People just love that story. As a matter of fact they love the idea so much they run with it. I remember telling one of my friends (who by the way has his PhD and is an ordained minister), and he just roared with laughter. He laughed so hard that he started to roll out of his chair; he was rocking

back and forth so much with laughter he started to cry. He could hardly compose himself. He would start to talk to make a comment and would just get overcome with amusement. Between his hysterics when he would gasp for air, I told him that some day I was going to put that in my book. He adamantly responded when he was able that I needed an entire chapter devoted to the subject. Also, he added that he and his wife were going to have so much fun with the concept. He knew of people in their lives who they just did not care for, and they were gonna have some pure enjoyment re-naming them. And, that half the fun was going to be coming up with just the right name. He was thankful for an idea that would channel some negativity into creativity.

As well I bet you, your family and your friends will enjoy coming up with some new pet names for your ex-spouse. My family has also been very creative in this game. My parents, who both speak fluent Italian, used some choice Italian words.

For those of you with children, this can be an important activity. When your children are old enough to use the cell phone and look for his name, it is better for them to find a real name than what you really want to call him. I think my children have asked me twice why their Dad's name is in my cell phone differently. I just nonchalantly stated that's what I call him. They have completely accepted it and ask no more questions.

In college, my persona was being formed to perfection. I had no idea this would become a survival skill of mine. I had gone to speak with one of my female professors. I wanted a woman's point of view for entering the work force and being a mother. In speaking with her, I explained that school had

always been difficult for me. I knew that the classroom atmosphere was not how I learned. My mother was a schoolteacher and understood that there were different learning styles and had always encouraged me to find the way I learned best. Upon hearing this, she abruptly stopped me. She told me that if I needed tutors or other help, I would never make it and I should not even try. Needless to say my mother was furious when I told her. After thinking about the conversation, I just renamed her…well…I renamed her in my less than grown-up attitude…"Dr. Fart Head" and began to find my way through college, then Physician Assistant School, eventually becoming a surgical Physician Assistant in Brain Surgery. I think I've learned a thing or two about change and persistence.

Now that I have shared this strategy, you need to be aware. Be aware if someone calls *you* by the wrong name again. It might not be because they forgot your name. How lovely that would be. Instead, it might be because you just got… renamed.

Ex-spouses and people who either purposely or inadvertently hurt our feelings are not the only things that need to be renamed. Certain objects and memories in our lives need to be relabeled or at the very least re-organized in our mind so we can recycle them for our future use.

We accumulate things throughout our lives. My house is no exception to this rule. I have made no formal study of all houses, but I dare say at the least, every house has a junk drawer. I might even go so far as to ask you to look in your purse, the back of your mini-van or SUV. I am a clean freak. Children have made me less obsessive; but clutter still bothers me. I believe as humans it is in our nature to gather and collect. Some do this more than others. Sometimes it is

for sentimental reasons, like Christmas cards or special gifts that have meaning. As we make our purchases or collect our treasures, we become attached whether by emotion, sentiment or for practical reasons. We can remember who gave it to us or where we bought or found it, if it was on sale, who was with us, what the weather was like, if our shoes hurt that day, if our hair was up or down, etc. Our minds are like a trap where all useless information hides. Sometimes we are unaware that we have all this information stored. That is until an event changes us, and how we feel about those objects.

Divorce, death, bad ex-bosses, poor decisions about money, or life in general, are all events that make us look back on information with bitterness or sorrow. When my father died I found it difficult to go into his room. It was hard to touch his clothes and smell them. I remember the first time I had to drive his truck. I held his personal set of car keys in my hand and just stood there rolling them in my hand over and over again, knowing he had touched them. One remembers the person with that object, event, or place, and it creates a memory.

Sometimes the memory is so strong you just want to avoid the material object or place all together. After a break-up of any kind have you had a hard time going to your once favorite restaurant, listening to certain songs? How do you feel about that piece of jewelry that was given to you by that once special person who now just broke your heart? Do you still feel like wearing it? Or do you feel like smashing it into a million pieces? Do you have a house full of furniture with every room a memory? Around every corner is there a memory of what life had been like?

See how our material possessions can have a positive thought attached to them at one moment, and then an event happens and you would rather those items be burned to the ground than continue to be taunted by them with what could have been, what should have been? It is hard to look at them now, much less think of even using them again.

I assume you are not filthy rich (yet!). I suppose there are a small percentage of people who could afford to throw out a house full of furniture, wardrobes, cars, and jewelry. But for the rest of us, we have a method for dealing with these emotional memories.

The first thing to realize is that the item or place itself is not bad or useless, just the memory is. Only the memory associated with it can emotionally hurt you. The idea is to change the memory attached to it. You do this by being creative. It is actually fun. Let one of your friends borrow your jewelry for an evening, have someone new in your life sit with you on that sofa…or do something more than just sit (I don't know how you're going to be able to look at your sofa the same way again after that night)…wear that special dress out to a fundraiser. Let your car be used in the school parade, plan your girlfriend's baby shower at your once favorite restaurant. Let your girlfriend wear those diamond earrings on a first date. If appropriate, you wear those diamond earrings on a first date. If you have absolutely no ideas, at the very least, sell it or eBay-it, or have a garage sale and make some money off of it.

Create new memories from those bad choices. Investigate ways to remember old favorite restaurants, stores, vacation destinations, grocery stores, church pews, gyms, etc. Your "bad" choices have given you a wealth of knowledge. It is called the school of hard knocks. It gives you insight and

intuition for the rest of your life. If you have had a bankruptcy, I bet you now know how to protect your wealth. If you have been sued, I bet you know how to better protect yourself in the future. If your credit score is bad, I bet you know how it got that way and how to insure better scores down the road. You are busting at the seams with information. The key is to use your knowledge as wisdom. If that means you need to rename your bankruptcy "my Bill Gates experience" to repackage it into a positive thought when you look back on it, do so.

And, there is more re-labeling that can be done. Did your grandmother ever say or have you ever heard the old expression "For heaven's sake, don't throw the baby out with the bath water!" I *think* she meant, keep the good things in your life, but get rid of the bad parts. At first, many times, one does not want to admit there was anything good in the now crumbled marriage. And even if there was good, sometimes we are too angry to admit it. We would rather just deny it. Now, I am here to say that is just foolishness. There were funny things that happened and even good things or the marriage would never have taken place.

One of my friend's who was contemplating a divorce from her husband one night discussed this very issue. Her husband thought them soul mates because of all the good things that had happened since they got married. My friend thought the good things that had happened since they got married were just the by-products of any two people working together to try and better each other. Either way, both did not like the turn their marriage had taken, but both were able to see there was good in the marriage. A perfect example of good from a marriage is the children. I could not think of a better gift or blessing. If you have been blessed in this way, do take time to cherish that fact.

Renaming your ex-spouse was easy and finding ways to remember physical items or places is a breeze when compared with the next part. What does one do with those good moments, funny times, knowledge gained and shared together? You cannot just throw those out with the bath water. But how do you rename, remember them without having painful memories? Once again, a little creativity is your friend.

Let me give an example by using one of my friend's who was getting divorced. While she was still married, her husband taught her to use the Internet to locate and reserve fancy hotels for cheap. That was a learned skill. She found it very difficult to use this Internet site while she was getting divorced due to the memories associated with it. Then we realized the site was a very useful tool and why waste the knowledge? By the way, our first girls' trip, we stayed at a great hotel for really cheap and laughed about it throughout our vacation. So you see the idea is to exploit the good, use it to your advantage and walk away from all the bad experiences and feelings attached to it. When it comes to more abstract ideas, knowledge or in this case a learned skill, it takes a little more creativity. Just remember all the same rules apply, but sometimes you gotta think outside the box on those.

Thinking of all the ways you have been hurt, derailed, or put down does nothing for what you want to become. Neither does thinking about those poor choices or what feels like bad mistakes along the way. The mind must first think it, before it can become a reality. Don't waste your time on what should have or could have been. Start thinking about what you want to create. Your brain makes the images in your head and then your body starts to fulfill that new world

you have created. Take the good, the bad and the ugly in your life, but recycle, reclaim and rebuild. Move forward with what can be.

It takes a little imagination, but it starts with positive thinking and speaking. It is helpful to create a world of optimism. It is not just being a "Pollyanna." You are taking action. You are mentally challenging yourself and physically doing things to better your world. Who better to take charge of your life than you? Just this step puts you back in the driver's seat. You will probably have many more ingenious ways to deal with your specific situation. You empower yourself. These are the first few steps to independence and expanding your thoughts and world. Remember, it does not mean bad things won't continue to happen to you, or you won't have any more bad days. It just means you now are creating ways to deal with everyday situations. At this point, I say, "I dare ya to give me a bad day. I'll just make it into a new good memory."

I was married for just shy of ten years. It took time for me to "wipe-out" the memories of my old way of life. I could not rename or re-memory everything; sometimes time is just the key. I remember when I was first divorced, I thought about my old way of life…too much. Then slowly my new life crept in and took precedence. Now, I only think about it when something triggers my mind. However, it is more like a thought about a dream.

For example, when you were in high school, the events that were taking place at that time probably seemed so important. If you are old enough to have at least had a high school reunion or like me, several high school reunions, you know those events are not pressing anymore. As a matter of fact, if you can even remember them, they may seem a

little ridiculous. I even know people who are now good friends but hardly knew each other in high school. They tell me they can't even remember the reason they didn't get along in high school.

I have heard it said that as a general rule it will take one half the length of time one is in a relationship to get over that relationship. For example, if you were dating someone for a year and then you broke up for whatever reason, in theory, it would take you six months to get over that person. I do not know if that is true or not, you can think back on your past relationships and put it to the test. Sometimes you can do all the cute little mind games and tricks you want, but sometimes time is just the key.

From time to time my daughter voices that she wishes she still had her original "Boo." Little does she know that when his first piece of shiny soft material fell off, I saved it. I took a picture of her with her "original" Boo. And, I am going to frame the picture with that piece of lost fabric and give it to her. As far as Boo is concerned, he is a good memory and in no fear of being renamed by anyone. Even her big brother knows no one messes with Boo.

Chapter 4

JUST TURN THE PAGE

My first boss after I was divorced told me to get ready to "climb my mountain!" With that being said, he gave me a sermon on a CD to listen to. The preacher on the CD explained that everyone has his or her mountain to climb/crisis to overcome. I liked the word picture of climbing a difficult mountain. I could relate the trials of divorce and the aftermath of divorce as the climb. I could even visualize what it would be like to reach the summit and look back at the path taken. But even more than that, I craved the view from the top. My boss had been divorced and understood how hard that was, but he also knew that my life was just beginning. Basically, divorce is hard but sometimes it is the beginning of your next great adventure. I came to understand my divorce was just the foothills; my life was the mountain I was about to climb. Also, I realized that divorce was not the final crisis I would ever have. I had to let go of the past to start again. But how do you let go when you feel so lost and devastated? How do you reconcile in your mind that you have put so much into going in one direction in your life and now not only must you let go of that, but find a new way. It is a bit daunting.

Just lay the whole truth out there to be scrutinized. I know there were things I could have changed; I could be specific in things I could have changed. However, it got to the point, I didn't care. I was actually glad for a way out of the marriage. That being said, it still does not change the fact

that at this point I must be transparent with my own feelings and honest with what had been going on to be able to move on from the ruined marriage. This allowed me, and will allow you, the ability to close that chapter of your life and to let go.

I have read that when people criticize it is actually a mirror image of what they truly feel of themselves. It is their way of making themselves feel more secure. Have you taken on anyone's unfair criticism? My friends who knew me before I was married, during my marriage and now after the marriage have seen the transformation in me. They saw me go into my marriage as a strong determined young lady and then come out the other end of the marriage with little self-esteem and poor self-confidence. With the aids in this book, my friends, and family, I pulled myself out of that train of thought.

At this point, I could explain the unraveling of my marriage. I could describe it in such detail that one could feel the raw emotions one goes through in a divorce. However, I will concisely say events began to escalate. Until one night I saw red. All the pieces of the puzzle came together. The denial stage was over for me. I was done.

However, it took me some time to realize my responsibility in the whole issue as well. But it is that realization that is the part of the truth you need to get. It may be easy for you to see what your soon to be ex-husband has done. It may be apparent by now the non-verbal cues you were getting. You may even be able to see the lack of remorse or worse the justification of behaviors. But do you see your role? What did you allow or when did you choose to look the other way? I am not saying what he did was appropriate or right. What I am saying is realize maybe you should have walked away years ago. Maybe, you should have listened when others

first had suspicions. How were you an enabler, per se? I reconcile it now only because I would not have had the children I have today, and I cannot imagine my life without them.

At one point, the elders of our church came to visit with me. I had the preacher of the church I had started attending and am now a member of come be with me at this "meeting." I remember one of the elders point blank say, "we are not going to take sides in this matter, because it is just a he said, she said matter." I calmly replied; "no, it is not a he said, she said matter." I said more, but I will protectively leave the rest of that conversation out of this discussion. The elder then said, "Well, you know God hates divorce." I squared myself off to him and looked him directly in the eyes and said, "There are a lot of other things that God clearly hates more."

They tried to persuade me with scripture not to get a divorce. However, with scripture, I showed my clear understanding of the rightful grounds I had. Our conversation was clear that I knew what I was talking about, scripturally, emotionally and physically. After the other men left, my preacher told me how proud he was of me for saying that. He told me, of course, God does not want people to get divorced, but clearly there are reasons for doing so. God even makes provisions for it. Even in strict Christian beliefs, there are exceptions to rules.

Before you can start this cleanup process, you must give yourself permission to let go. Sometimes, we fight for so long, and so hard, we forget to stop fighting. The holding on can feel like an addiction and can be just as difficult to release. There comes a point when you have done everything you can. Every possibility has been exhausted. Many times the problem is not your willingness to resolve

issues.   You don't have to keep going on and on, hitting your head against a wall.   Did it ever cross your mind that maybe letting go could be the best possible action?   Now, if there is more for you to do, work on, or other steps you can take, do it.   You don't want to walk away from a job half done.   Doing that could leave you feeling empty, guilty and remorseful.   By all means research every nook and cranny, for sanity's sake.

Were boundaries crossed in your marriage?   Once boundaries have been crossed the first time, it is easier for a person to cross them again and again.   Be fully aware that other people in our lives make choices that affect us.   But, it is time for you to make a choice.   Are you going to forgive, again, with the high probability that as before, those boundaries will be crossed another time?

I needed to know without a doubt I had done everything I could in my power to save the marriage.   At that point, I realized enough was enough! It was and is okay to focus on productive issues.   You can only beat a dead horse for so long.   I realize change was not possible for my marriage, but a better realization was that *I* could change.   I was in charge of stopping the insanity that had been created.

Letting go may be your first step.   For others, getting out of bed is the first step.   Don't stick your head in the sand like an ostrich anymore.   Instead, be fully aware of your surroundings and what is happening.   You are just going through change.   Admittedly, a big change, but you can still transform into a new normal.   It will be frightening at times, refreshing at others.   That's life. And whether you feel like it or not, you have to get out of bed to experience even the revitalizing parts.   You can learn to stay focused on the thrilling and leave the negative in the dust.   You can learn to

blow right through obstacles as you reach for your new goals. Keep in mind, everyone's emotional timetable and schedule of events is different. Decide not to rush through your process of healing or you will cheat yourself of growth. At first your divorce will be on your mind like an obsession. You will learn ways to take a break from the memories that bite and rip at your soul. You will find life is exhilarating! Just turn the page.

On the vadeninc.com web site you can even get a "Letting Go" certificate. The certificate is free to you. You can use it to release yourself from your current life. It can represent your new life, your change, and your first step to independence. It is empowering!

Once you have given yourself permission to let go, you need some solid ideas of how to do so. Often, what happens is we get caught in our minds. Our world seems to be changing all around us, but we continue to think of the past. We may start out setting our minds on moving forward, but our minds keep wandering back to what went on before. It feels like you are working against yourself. You are. There needs to be clear-cut activities to do to relieve the tension in your brain and allow you to move into flow of thought. Sometimes our minds don't let us do that. Moving forward in every facet of your life is not something that just happens. Getting your divorce decree in hand is an end physically. However, we are talking about beginnings. We need action that will move us both physically and mentally in a positive direction.

You can start by having a divorce party. Another friend of mine and I were getting a divorce at the same time. One of our mutual friends threw a divorce party for us. We spent weeks planning it and talking about it. We had all agreed on

a specific night for the gala to take place. We talked about burning something that reminded us of our exes and how good that would feel. But then we decided that put too much emphasis on the past and this party was not about looking back, it was about moving forward without them as a part of our lives. My friend could do this a little easier than I could because she had not had children. My ex was always going to be attached, but that didn't mean I could not banish him from the rest of my life.

We planned an evening of fun activities. Dinner, friends and fun were the venue. My friend had made each of us a personal cake with special frosting and appropriate happy divorce cake sayings on each cake. We celebrated our freedom that night. We celebrated our new beginning that night. You see letting go does not need to be scary or painful…it can be fun.

Another way to let go is to let in nature. Bringing nature into your life can be very calming. I will admit I am not an outdoorsy person. I don't like to go camping. As a matter of fact, I don't even understand the concept of camping. I don't understand why you would work so hard to create a warm inviting cozy home with a lovely kitchen, a dining room, a great big TV, a luscious mattress to sleep on and a sparkling clean, fresh bathroom with big fluffy towels just to go outside and sleep in the dirt with all the bugs and varmints. I obviously just don't get it. Now if you call taking a bathing suit and a toothbrush to a ritzy beach resort camping…I'm in. I say I like four walls, a roof and a thermostat. But that doesn't mean I don't enjoy nature. If you are an outdoorsy type, this suggestion is probably even more in tune with you. You definitely will need to arrange more time in the outdoors.

But, for the rest of us who don't enjoy the bug spray or varmints there are other ways to enjoy nature. Go have a picnic. I have done this with my children. It is so much fun to pull the picnic basket down and declare a picnic day. It is so much fun trying to find what fits and won't spill in your basket. We have had Pet Shop animals and Ben 10 characters make our picnic basket, as well as other items I would never have thought to take with us. You don't even have to drive anywhere. My children and I have sat outside our front door and had picnics. If you don't have children, go for a picnic and take some magazines or a good book to read. I say magazines, because I remember when I was going through my divorce, my attention span was about two minutes. Try sitting under a tree and feel the wind on your face. Try different trees; just get outside, even for a moment.

Go camping if this is something you have liked in the past or think you would like to try, build a fire, and roast some hot dogs and marshmallows. If you have children, you can camp in your living room. One time we bought a pop-up tent and then took more sheets and expanded our tent. We still had hotdogs and s'mores. We did not end up sleeping in our new pop-up tent; everyone decided they wanted a mattress. I was so glad.

At night try catching fireflies. I confess I don't like bugs, and my children know that birds creep me out with their eyes on the side of their heads that go blink, blink, blink. But we still found ways to enjoy the calming effects of the outdoors.

I also don't like it too hot, and I definitely don't like it too cold, so I don't spend gross amounts of time outside. Luckily for me (and my neighbors), I live where we pay for our lawns to be maintained. My children call me a plant murderer. I have

managed to kill houseplants, outdoor plants; even a cactus has no chance with me. We have fake plants in our home, and I try to smother them with a good layer of Oklahoma dust. But that doesn't stop me from enjoying nature. I bring in freshly cut flowers either from my mother's garden, because you know I couldn't grow them, or I purchase a five-dollar bunch from the grocery store. In the fall I have the children gather pinecones, and we put them in crystal bowls. For Thanksgiving or Christmas, I have the children take the pine cones, role them in glue and different colored glitter and stick them back in the crystal bowls for a beautiful table centerpiece. My children bring me dandelions in the summer that I proudly display in cups of water.

One sunny day my son and I sat and watched a trail of ants. Those ants worked so hard. He and I became intrigued by those little guys. We started to put out different sizes of crumbs to watch them find the crumbs, attack them and eventually carry those crumbs off. We put cups down as obstacles and action figures to see if they would maneuver around them or just how they would react. We were mesmerized for hours. My children and I used to draw outside on the sidewalk with chalk. Then we would wet the sidewalk down with the hose and draw with wet chalk. Outside activities do not have to be elaborate or complicated. When one is going through a divorce, the simple things can be the best.

One of the best ways to learn how to let go is to stop thinking about how pathetic your life is. Make an effort to help someone else in need. Go volunteer your time at a shelter, be a part of your church benevolence program. Help with Vacation Bible School at your church. Spend an hour in your child's classroom helping the teacher. This requires no money, just a few hours of your time.

Once a year one of my friends anonymously sends one hundred dollars to someone in need. She watches all year round to see who is going to be the beneficiary of this gift. She gets a charge out of helping someone and them having no idea who gave them the money. Ironically, at the time when my friend started doing this she could have used a few anonymous checks sent to her. But she would save up the hundred dollars through out the year to give to someone else. She realized she got more out of it than they did. Doing for others no matter what your circumstances will change your perspective on the world and your life. You are important and needed by others. You will gain much objectivity on your life while doing these activities.

Here is an amusing one. Let go by using "both sides." Use both sides of the bed, the vanity, and the closet; use both sides of the garage. Stop looking at the emptiness and fill it up with something useful or fun. At first I couldn't decide on which side of the bed to sleep. I would try one side for a night and the other side the next. Both had their pros and cons. One side was closer to the bathroom. The other side seemed softer. I couldn't make up my mind and wondered why I had to. I started alternating the sides of the bed. I now sleep in the middle of my big king-sized bed. And if a side wins out, it usually is the one closer to the bathroom.

When I moved into my new home, I had my bathroom remodeled. It had been built back in the eighties. There were low tile countertops, no good storage, one sink; the entire room was very dated looking. When I redesigned it I obviously put in more storage and used beautiful granite countertops and added another sink. Nowadays, most want two sinks in the master bathroom. Someday, I might want to sell my current residence. But for now, I have two sinks, one

I use, one that remains empty, staring at me every day. I had to fill up the emptiness. I now use one side of the vanity for putting on make-up and the other for holding my mail. Now that my daughter is getting older, she and I have enjoyed getting ready to go out side-by-side.

I used to daily switch the sides of the garage where I would park. I now keep the other side clear for my guests on rainy or snowy days. My guests are able to pull right up into a dry clean spot and make their way easily into my home. It makes me feel like such a great hostess. One side of my closet is for summer items and the other is for winter clothes. I will have to make a few adjustments if I ever remarry. I will cross that bridge when I come to it. At one point, I even had my children's clothes in my closet so it made folding and ironing quicker. As a single mom, you do whatever you can to make life easier on yourself. The "both sides" game is fun. Don't get trapped into one way of thinking.

Let go by listening. Listen to what other people have to say. It seems that when a woman becomes pregnant others think it is appropriate for them to touch her belly. I would never just walk up to another woman, or man for that matter, and place my hand on her abdomen. I don't know what makes people think it is okay during pregnancy. The same is true when you go through a divorce. Well, they don't place their hand on your belly, but they think it is appropriate to tell you just what they think of your ex. At first you feel a little defensive, even if what they are saying is true. It's only because it seems a bit overwhelming and you feel like an idiot, because you did not see it earlier yourself. But let's be honest, love is blind. Once you get over the initial shock, listen to what they have to say. People will surprise you. When I was married my impression was that all our friends liked us because they thought my ex-husband was so

wonderful. The truth was many were our friends because of the money and big-boy toys he had. After the divorce people whom I highly respected, even people I hardly knew would tell me things that made my jaw drop. People really can see through nonsense. Sometimes you just need to listen.

I then surrounded myself with good people. Once I felt safe again, I started to let go of my past by once again listening to what those people thought of my abilities and me. The lesson is to know who you are, be in control of your emotions resulting in control of your life. Do not carry the weight of someone else's faults or misgivings. We all have enough faults of our own to deal with, without adding false ones to our picture. Work through your faults and build on your strengths. You will become stronger through all your experiences. You never have to allow another human being to degrade you or make you feel less of yourself. It took me some time, but I know who I am and who I strive to be.

Now, be careful, because, your natural instinct will be to spill the beans. You will want to shout from the mountaintops all that has been done wrong to you. You will want to scream justification. But wait, sometimes saying nothing speaks louder than words. People are naturally curious, but you don't have to tell every detail or answer all questions. The more people continue to ask about the divorce the more it keeps you thinking about the past. It is okay to tell people it is not appropriate to "touch your belly." Once people stop asking about the divorce and start asking about your new career, new house, new endeavors, you can let go.

Be ready with a quick answer for prying questions. A good comeback, if appropriate, is, "Well he has made choices God does not expect me to live with." With that reply, most

people will get the picture and realize you're not talking. Come up with whatever you feel necessary to protect yourself. I am sure your attorney would agree another good reply might be, "my lawyer has advised me not to talk about it right now." Or, "it's too difficult to talk about right now." If you say your phrase enough times, people will stop asking. This will allow you to move into your future.

With that being said, you also need to learn to be a screener. People will intrude into your life from all angles in this day and age. Your phone is there for your convenience. It is not there for others to pop in when it is a good time for them. Once you answer the phone, some people will keep you all day. I do not know about you, but the time I have must be used wisely. Use your caller ID to your advantage. Also, set a time to turn off your computer. I used to hate opening emails. All I got was outlandish things to deal with from my lawyers. If I looked at my email throughout the day, I would end up stressing over each and every one. I made a rule for myself that I would check my email once, resolve the issues and not let other emails ruin my day.

Start by knowing your ex-spouse can no longer hurt you. What? You heard me, you cannot get hurt unless you allow it. If you let go of the past, he has lost his power over you. This was a big light bulb experience for me once I got it. I still smile when I think of the strength behind the idea. I loved him once, but I have the choice to not love him anymore. That chapter of my life is done. Just as I write this book, I see blank pages ahead with nothing but opportunity and creativity waiting to be explored. It is exciting.

Chapter 5

MIND TICKS!

As the doors are pushed open, the operating room has a hint of a chill. Scurrying around like ants is the best way to describe how we prepare for surgery. We each have particular, crucial jobs to do. Once the patient is in the room, prepped in sterile fashion, put to sleep with monitoring probes and our equipment in place, one can almost feel the pause in the air. Then the surgeon asks for the scalpel. As delegate as brain surgery is, there are many aspects that just seem barbaric in practice. I know why we do them and yet cramming pins in people's heads in order to keep those heads perfectly still seems cruel. Also, drilling burr holes in the skull to remove the scalp is the not-so-delicate side of my job. I am a neurosurgical Physician Assistant, and I first assist in brain surgery. One part of brain surgery that fascinates me is the removal of brain tumors. Many times the actual tumor will have a slight grayish tint to it compared with the color of the brain itself. The job of distinguishing between the two makes it tedious not to suck out good tissue vital for brain function.

Specific areas of brain function could be lost or altered, depending on where we must work in the brain. Some areas deal with the ability to recall past events, some deal with the ability to form thoughts into words, and other areas deal with your personality. Then there are the risks of the procedure. I think most people are overwhelmed at the idea of brain surgery. It always astounds me how people in the clinic will listen to the risks and possibilities of surgery and still, their

only questions will be about how long the incision will be and how much hair they will lose. Now, I have a lot of hair, I do understand, but losing part of my brain???

During surgery, we try not to touch the brain. This has always been hard for me, because I want to just put my finger on it and push a little. I want to feel the consistency. It is a bit like a hardboiled egg, maybe a little softer, and the color is more that of silly putty with a hint of yellow to it. I remember when I first started, I asked if I could touch it and my surgeon told me, "We try not to touch the brain." There are so many things we know about the brain and how it functions, but there are also so many things we just don't know. So, I resist and keep my cotton pickin' hands off the brain. However, I get a feel for it under the retractors.

So do we only use 10% of our brain? Working in neurosurgery debunks that myth for me. If we only used a small percentage of our brain then removing part of the brain would not be so detrimental. And in that case, I could poke it all I wanted. However, even when you are asleep not only do you dream, but your body continues to function. You may realize you are too hot or too cold so you flop a leg outside the covers, or you add the blanket at the foot of your bed. You feel your hand go to sleep, so you change positions. Or suddenly you realize you need to use the restroom. You may hear the rain hitting the window outside your bedroom. Your brain continues to use many areas and process information.

Actually, sometimes it would be nice to be able to turn your brain to silent. Maybe not completely turn your brain off, but, if one could stop thinking or obsessing over particular issues. This is where mind tricks can be valuable.

When you are in a crisis mode, such as a divorce, it is sometimes difficult to take your mind off of your problems. But for your inner self to survive you must take a mental break. I call this taking a "brain break." Many times if you can relax yourself, you can later face the problems with a renewed strength. This in turn will allow you to deal with the situation and sometimes even come up with solutions. All of that in theory sounds good, but some of us are obsessive worriers. Some of you even make up scenarios in your head of what could or might happen and then begin to worry about that. STOP, wait a minute. Let's start off easy.

First, allow yourself five minutes a day to take a "brain break." Now for those of you in the storm of divorce, I understand it is easier said than done to take your mind off of your issues for even a moment. You're going to have to trust and know intellectually that in five minutes you can go back and refocus on your troubles. During your designated five minutes you must do something and think about something other than your divorce problems. This means you will have to plan your five minutes. Your brain will not automatically stop thinking about your problems. You must redirect your thoughts and have something specifically in mind to think about or do. Call a friend, watch the news, write a letter, look for lost items, do a crossword puzzle, play the Wii. Do anything other than think about your problems. Keep in mind, five minutes off is difficult to accomplish in the midst of a divorce. Those of you who tend to obsess like this may find it useful to set a timer or use a stopwatch. But you will get better. Then as you become more comfortable with this exercise, extend the time. Now, if you are a procrastinator, don't abuse your "brain breaks" as a way to avoid dealing with your life at hand.

You can even take a "brain break" while driving. Obviously, do not take your mind off your driving. However, being alone in the car with your thoughts and the radio can drive you crazy. The radio just seems to know what songs to play to keep your thoughts on your "long ago." It will play sappy love songs when your heart has been trampled, it will play sad songs reminding you of yesterdays. However, there is a simple solution to help your mind. Here is the procedure...change the station.

When I was first divorced my drive to and from work was quite long. I learned to enjoy that time, because it gave me a transition between my work environment and my home life. I found the time it took to drive home allowed me to switch gears more easily from the go-go-go Physician Assistant and slow down to loving, caring Mom. However, at first, the time alone in my car wreaked havoc on my mind.

I almost dreaded the drive. After analyzing it further, I realized mentally, my drive home was easier than my drive to work. It was then I pieced together that on my way home, I thought about what I was going to make for dinner, what household chores I needed to do that night, how I was going to figure in my children's homework with balancing some family fun. I had no room in my brain for other problems.

My way to work was more difficult because the next few work hours were already planned for me. I had free time in my head to just think. I realized that the day of the week made a difference. Mondays were not so bad because I still had thoughts of what I had done that past weekend. Fridays weren't too bad either, because I was thinking of what my weekend plans were going to be. However, the rest of the week was hard. I worried about the "what ifs." I had conversations with people in my head. I would think about

what I would say to them and what idiots they had been. I struggled with the idea that my dream of a traditional family home life had been shattered for my children.

You need time to think about your problems, but not obsess about them. Quite frankly, I was just tired of thinking about *those* people. So, I decided I needed an ace up my sleeve. I needed something to think about on my drive Tuesday through Thursday. The other days of the week, Monday and Friday, were already covered. So I set out to create a diversion. It is my experience that it is even better if you can have several aces up your sleeve.

An ace gives you something else to think about. It takes your mind off of those repetitive thoughts. You need to be able to give yourself a break. That may sound obvious. This involves a bit of planning on your part. The trick is to know beforehand what your topics will be.

Here is the problem. If we get in that rut of thinking about our difficulties without knowing ahead of time what our ace is going to be, it is near impossible to think of anything else but our problems. It is like telling a kindergartener not to look at the puppy in the window. You know they cannot resist. They must look at the puppy in the window. Or try telling a teenage boy to stop thinking about the opposite sex. Impossible!

You must make sure your aces are easy topics. For example, think about what you did each day on your last vacation. Think about what you wore yesterday, last Sunday to church, what you had for breakfast or what gifts you need to buy for Christmas. Can you remember something significant for each year you have been alive? What is your very first memory of life? What was your favorite birthday?

The list is endless. The key is to already have a few ideas on which you can focus. Each time your mind drifts and it will, refocus on your ace.

Sometimes, we need a reminder to shift our thoughts. While still in college, a friend of mine could never remember to turn off her headlights before getting out of her car. The outcome was always a dead car battery. To remedy the situation, she stuck a yellow, sticky post-it note on her steering wheel. She seemed to be a bit embarrassed by it, but I always thought it ingenious. We can even use that same clever idea and put a post-it note on the steering wheel to remind us to turn off our brains from a certain subject. You could even write your aces on the sticky. Just take care when driving.

Another time to use a "brain break" is when you are drifting off to sleep. One of the most difficult times to stop thinking about your terrible situation is when you are trying to fall asleep. You can mull over in your brain so long what needs to be done, should have been done, might happen, etc. Again, having done some pre-planning to know where to direct your thoughts prior to falling asleep is important. Some more suggestions include trying to focus on a room in your house. In your mind, re-arrange the furniture, choose new wallpaper or pick a new paint color, add lamps, plants and throw pillows. Imagine the new colors and textures you have created in your mind. Try making your room a different style than what you would actually choose. For example, if you like French Country style, think up a retro-modern look for your room. Once that room is completed, move to another.

If you can't even imagine turning off the lights and attempting to shut your eyes yet, have some magazines

handy. Even junk mail catalogs will do. Go through those and pick out items you like. Create a wish list from the pages of the magazines. This way you can train your brain to think of something else before going to sleep. Allow your brain to rest so your other body parts can rest, too.

Another suggestion for "brain breaks" is the following: if you are lying awake in the dark, try imagining what it would be like if you could only live in one room of your house. For example, if you could only live in your kitchen, where would you put your bed? If you have children, would you let them sleep on top of the cabinets? How would they climb up and what would you add to make it safe? Where would the computer go? Where would you put your clothes? Or, think about what if you had to live in your parents' home, your friend's home. How would you decorate it differently, if at all? How would you rearrange their furniture? Where would you put your furniture if their furniture were not there? What route would you take to work if you lived at their homes?

The possibilities go on and on without limits. Just remember it takes practice to stay focused. Don't get upset with yourself when you find you have traveled in your mind back to your problems. Your problems are real, and you are justified in needing to spend thought-provoking time on those problems. Just know it will take some effort to learn to shut those thoughts off for a while to be able to get some well-deserved rest. Every time you find your mind wandering back to your worries, force yourself back to your mind project. This will create a more restful night, which in turn will make for a more productive day.

Even if you do not have the money or time to actually get away on a trip, plan one anyway. This can help deviate from your constant thoughts for a break. Decide where you want

to go. Ask people who have already been there about good restaurants, good sites to see, or maybe what they would recommend or steer clear of the next time they went. Do your research on the best time of year to go to your destination. Plan your outfits or the specific clothing you will need. If you are planning to go somewhere warm, you may need a bathing suit. Get online or look at your mail catalogs for the best one. If you are planning on the mountains, search for your gear, online or use mail catalogs. Find the best prices on hotels, airfare and car rentals. If your journey is to a foreign speaking place, learn a few important phrases in that language. You may even learn to converse in that language. None of this requires a great amount of investment or too much effort. The exercise is fun and gets you in the mode of thinking about your future. It also gives you one of those "brain breaks" we all need.

Another "brain break" idea without breaking the bank is going to the movies. A movie ticket plus popcorn, candy and a drink can seem expensive. However, it is not as expensive as some other activities. Don't forget you could always rent a movie at home and make your own popcorn and buy candy at the store. During a movie you can let your mind get lost. It is easy to get caught up in a storyline or begin to identify with a character. Movies can even be inspiring to you. They can show you how other characters in the story deal with situations and life problems. Movies can give you a different view on your way of thinking. It does not mean you have to accept or agree with the message, but it helps to get you off a one-way thought process.

When I was going through my divorce, I enjoyed "Out of Africa." To me it dealt with basic human struggles and the stages of life. I identified with "Under the Tuscan Sun." I enjoyed "Sense and Sensibility" and "Hope Floats," which

both renewed my soul for the possibility to love again. Another period piece I liked was "The Duchess." It was interesting to see how women of the time dealt with infidelity and the social restraints and economic immobility placed on them. If all those sound too serious, I also enjoyed "The Princess Bride" with my children. I was able to laugh through many children movies. I was able to escape my world for a while with laughter.

Other inexpensive ideas include going to a museum. You can get lost walking around the displays and exhibits. Here in Oklahoma City, we have a wonderful place called the National Cowboy and Western Heritage Museum. My children love visiting for the day. They have an old town built inside the museum. My children love going to see the town with the wagons on the streets, the jail and the shops. There is even a church. The children took turns standing behind the pulpit preaching or leading us in song. There is another area that the children could dress up with cowboy boots, hats and chaps. There is camp equipment and tents set up to play both inside and out. There are sponge logs for building cabins and whatever else the children could dream of creating. The grounds are pretty as well with meandering paths lined with Oklahoma grasses and plants. There are ponds with fish swimming and much more to see.

One time while I was at work, my mother took my children and one of their friends to the museum. They exhausted themselves till lunchtime. Fortunately, the museum had a café. One of the options on the menu was English Tea. The four of them decided to order this to further their adventure that day. They had scones and little cucumber sandwiches and a bundle of fun. My mother had told me of their great day, and the children showed off their treasures they had purchased at the gift store. Later that evening while I was

cooking dinner my daughter was drawing at the kitchen table. In my best English accent I asked my daughter "did you like your tea today?" Still in an English accent I continued, "I understand you had crumpets and scones…" I was interrupted by my daughter who turned around, looked at me and said, "stop speaking Spanish, Mom." Ever since then, whenever someone uses any kind of accent, someone always blurts out "stop speaking Spanish." So you see, even a trip to a local museum can create memories and supply educational entertainment not just for you, but for your children as well. You do not have to compete with money; just learn to use it wisely.

Another idea is the library. I am aware you can do most things on the Internet these days. However, for some of us, we want and need to just get out of the house. We may not be quite ready for a big social engagement but would like to do something, anything. Sounds strange, but going to the library can refocus your mind, and the best part is that it is free. You can get immersed in so many different ideas. You can look up subjects of interest or subjects you know nothing about. You can find a novel to read or how-to books. If your attention span is too short, go to the periodicals, read Oprah's magazine or "SELF," a parenting magazine, you can even sit and people watch. The idea is to expand and open up our world by using resources we did not know were available to us.

Holidays can be difficult emotionally. The demands can get even harder when you add children to the mix. They end up celebrating every holiday including their birthdays twice, once at Dad's and once at home with me. We decided in our household this would be treated as a blessing. Furthermore, I have never tried to one up my ex-husband on vacations, birthday parties or any other monetary endeavor. My

children and I do as we please in our family and have created some of the most memorable times of my life. Having to start thinking of new traditions can give you a 'brain break."

One year for Thanksgiving we decided to dress the part. I was a pilgrim with my black shawl wrapped around my shoulders. My son dressed as an Indian. He made himself a headdress with feathers stapled to the back. He used face paints and applied war paint. My daughter was a pink ballet-dancing pilgrim. I am not sure if they had pink ballet-dancing pilgrims then but we went with it. We had so much fun eating our turkey and stuffing that year. If I remember correctly, I did not have the children on Thanksgiving Day that year, but we celebrated our hearts out the week before the actual day.

Another holiday tradition we have is decorating the Christmas tree, over and over and over again. I always dreamed and had planned in my mind that when I got married and had children I would enjoy decorating for Christmas. In my mind's eye, I would have a small tree in each of the children's rooms for them to decorate themselves. Then I would have other trees perfectly placed around the house displaying different themes I had chosen. I would hang mistletoe and bring in freshly cut bows to lie across the mantle top. All of that has yet to happen. Instead, since my children were small they would put the ornaments on the tree and then the next day remove the ornaments and put them all back on in different places. They both love to do this. The most outlandish tree to date had a pirate hat on top instead of a star or angel.

Christmas does not just have to be about how much you spend on gifts. Instead create holiday moments and

memories. Go to the big department stores and see how they have decorated for the holidays. Drive to a downtown area and see what decorations they used. Grab some hot chocolate with friends or your children and drive by the neighborhoods that have holiday lights up in the yards. One of my friends always finds ways to drive down Santa Fe Street on Christmas, because it has Santa in the name. These are all ideas to get you started thinking how to refocus.

My children have yet to say, "Hey Mom, remember that toy you got me for Christmas?" Yes, my children are grateful for the toys and love unwrapping them just as much as any child. However, what they do say and remember are things like, "Are we going to make gingerbread houses again"…"Do we get to make ornaments again"…"Do you remember when the blue glitter glue shot across the kitchen?" (And then we all look up to see if we still have some remnants of blue glitter on the kitchen shutters where it blasted out of the bottle.)

My children love the fact that no matter how many walls get painted or re-painted in our home, their growth chart will never be painted over. The beginning of every school year, I measure the children using the good old back-against-the-wall, heels-to-the-edge, stand-flat-footed, book-on-the-head way. It is dated with their name. It is these gatherings of small moments and rituals that are far more valuable to your family; more valuable than silver, gold or money. But you have to come up with them for your family.

The positive side of divorce, is that you do not have someone else there to tell you that you can't do something a certain way. You are not bound by their inability to bend from their own ideas. You alone or you and your children

get to decide on the traditions to keep and the new ideas to incorporate. This makes every holiday or event special and unique to your family.

I cannot emphasize enough this next activity for a "brain break." Exercise, exercise, exercise! My medical background teaches that exercise helps to release endorphins, which help to improve mood. Take a walk around the block, try some roller skates or roller blades, go to the ice rink, shoot some hoops, join a gym, get a trainer, take a hike, ride a bike, go dancing, play some golf. Just get moving, and keep moving every day. Breathe in some good air and let it out. Exercise is a stress reliever. I have noticed that when I stop exercising my brain seems foggy. I feel like I cannot think through problems. When I take myself for a run, miraculously my thoughts clear and I am back to problem solving. Besides, the results of exercise don't look so bad on your body either. And that is just some food for thought to prepare you for dating. But, that's another book.

Enlist your friends to be your health guru. Let them come over and clean out your freezer of ice cream and your pantry of potato chips. Maybe you're someone who doesn't eat during crisis. Let your friends stock your refrigerator with healthy foods. You probably could manage to munch on a few carrots, grapes or toast. Even if you just can't sit or stomach a full-fledged meal, eat something. I always tell my friends I lose the most weight on my "D" diets; Death and Divorce diets, none of which are very appealing or easy.

It is exhausting to tell all the people who are in your life everything that is happening. Sometimes you need a break from the daily chores that are required during a crisis. It is physically impossible to take care of every task that is needed throughout a crisis. It is helpful to surround yourself

with people who care and want to help. Assign someone to be your spokesperson. This person is someone who helps call certain people to share and report facts. Assign another person to be your health guru. Let this person take you on walks, and make sure you are actually eating. Allow someone to be your legal advisor. Let that person go with you to all-important meetings. It is always good to have an extra pair of ears to help remember things. But be cautious whom you choose.

Sometimes we just need a break from making the decisions. There are some points in life we need to learn to lean on our friends. Sometimes we need our friends just to see our need and step in and help us out a bit. At one point, life was becoming too hectic. I had about ten things on my plate and was unable to get anything accomplished. I felt like my life was just spinning. My friend took me to dinner. He tried to make pleasant conversation, but I could hardly put sentences together. As I searched for words, he stopped me mid-breath. He pulled out a piece of paper and said, "Go, tell me everything that is bothering you!" I started in on my first problem and tried to discuss it. He stopped me again and said he just wanted a list; we would deal with each of them individually. I started again with the list. At the end he asked if there was anything else that needed to be put on the list. I shook my head, overwhelmed at the length of the list. He then proceeded at the top of the list and we came up with solutions for each item; even an order in which certain tasks needed to be done. I figured how grand, and while I was with him, I felt calm. But I was concerned that my feeling of worry would flood in again once I was away from him. Once I was home, I started to feel that since of urgency creep in, but for some reason I stuffed my hands in my jacket pocket. My hand felt the list. I pulled it out and saw all our notes and well thought-out plans. I began to cry,

not because I knew it was going to be okay, but because someone had taken the time to acknowledge my fears and help me work through them. I had a friend who understood me and knew what I needed to continue functioning in my life. Find someone you respect who you can bounce ideas off of. Sometimes the act of just saying your frustrations out loud is helpful with someone you can trust.

There are coffee breaks, smoke breaks, spring breaks and now "brain breaks." These mind tricks allow you some much-needed rest from your thoughts. It may take some time to train you to refocus. When you notice your thoughts have drifted back onto your problems, use your aces to re-direct to a different subject. The nice thing about "brain breaks" is that with this procedure there is no incision and no hair loss.

Chapter 6

GRIEF IS DRIVING AND ANGER IS HANGING OUT THE BACK WINDOW!

When I started running I thought my lungs were going to collapse, my heart was going to abandon my chest for relief and my legs would forever feel like rubber bands. I must admit I started running for all the wrong reasons. I told myself it was to prove I had become a strong woman and could run a half marathon. I had always dreamed of running a full marathon and thought maybe I could start with a half and then move up to a full. But to be truthful, it was because I met a man who was planning on running the marathon. I fell for his charm and warmth. I was so impressed by his determination, not just with the marathon, but also for life in general. He taught me that running though physical was also a mental game. I began to train. I found that on the days I did not run, I felt more fatigued and generally less well equipped to deal with life. Further, I developed a since of confidence in myself with each additional mile that I would add to my course.

I will never forget the day of the Memorial Marathon. It was a beautiful crisp morning in Oklahoma. My longest run had

only been ten miles. That day I had to add an additional three miles. By the tenth mile, I was exhausted and my legs ached as my feet pounded the pavement. I kept running. Along the route my father would be there to cheer me on and then he would drive a little farther to get out and encourage me some more. I ran through neighborhoods; I kept running. I ran along business roads; I kept running. I wanted to stop and give up; I kept running. I finally came around the last corner and could spot the finish. My friend, who had long since finished the race, came up beside me and started running with me. We ran together for just a little way. Now with every stride pain came up through my feet and shot through my thighs. I was hot and sweaty. My i-pod had long since run through my play-list. There were no more inspiring songs of strength to sustain me anymore. Then he told me to dig in deep and sprint the rest of the way across the finish line. He left me at that point to finish the race by myself, so I could feel the accomplishment on my own. I am forever grateful to him for allowing me that moment. I have carried that feeling of success with me ever since. I did not start out running for the right reasons, but I ended up at the finish line with all the right ones. I have not run a full marathon yet, and training a few years later to do another half marathon, I injured my foot badly. However, I still run or walk because I know the good feeling I get from the activity. It helps me deal with everyday stresses and anger that still creeps into my life. In turn, I know I look better and stay in shape. Exercise will help boost your immune system, build energy and keep you strong for, heaven forbid, your next crisis.

Realize, anger and sorrow will come. It is inevitable. It is just part of the process. A family friend who is a psychologist gave wise counsel to one of my friends going through divorce. My friend continued on and on, lamenting about her

past. After some time of this, he finally told her "you have worn your tragedy clothes long enough, you can change clothes now." I have thought of that often. In the Bible it talks of those in mourning. It describes them as tearing their clothes and putting ash or sackcloth on their heads. They would observe this ritual for a period of time. Then one day the mourning process would symbolically be over. They would get up and put on their regular clothes. We have a similar practice in our society. We wear black or dark clothing to funerals. We consider a year to be a "normal" grieving period. I thought of my own divorce. There did seem to be a period of time when I wore my "divorce" clothes. I even lived in "tragedy town" in my tragedy clothes with my tragedy gas station and tragedy grocery store and on and on it went. But then a day came when I mentally took off my tragedy clothes. You have the power to do that. No one is keeping you in your tragedy uniform but you.

Grief is a process and so is healing from a divorce. I have watched some of my friends going through divorce, and they tried to fast track themselves through the stages, or ignore their true emotions. I have seen them treat their broken marriages as a break-up from a bad boyfriend. I have seen them act smug and quickly enter back into the dating scene as a method of emotionally nursing themselves back to health. This approach can backfire. However hard you try, you cannot look right through the fact that your marriage was broken. You must *feel it* to *heal it*. If you rush through your emotions, you will not learn from the experience. Just covering up or replacing your feelings with new ones can haunt you later. When you least expect it, your old painful emotions will resurface and most likely mess something up in your future. You may have been the problem, you may not have been the problem, but you were there. Now is the time to deal with and discover what must be put to rest.

Most of us don't wake up one morning and say here comes my divorce crisis! I am going to brace myself and weather the storm. Now, do not get me wrong, there are crises like that. For example, my father's death was like that. I lost my father one summer to a sudden massive heart attack. Intellectually, I knew it was better to lose him in an instant. He would not have tolerated a long drawn out death process well. I still grieved. And even though I mourned, and still mourn my father's death, I cannot imagine my mother's grief. She lost the one who chose her and adored her. They were "one" for fifty-one years. She grieved. But also, she tried at first to grieve my loss, too. She knew the loss I had suffered from my ex-husband and now bore the loss of my father. Then she realized she could not grieve for me. She had to grieve, and she had to allow me to go through my process of sorrow. Unfortunately, she could not take that from me. She came to understand I had to go through each step of the grief process, too. Though my father's death was sudden and unexpected, I knew I had to put on my emotional seat belt and travel the road of grief.

However, there are many other difficulties in life, which leave us bewildered and confused. We must allow ourselves the time to reflect and heal. The steps in the grieving process allow us that space.

Divorce has its own progression of grief and within that pathway is the inevitable anger point. One of the stages of grief specifically is anger. What do you do with your anger when it comes? Notice I used the word "when." It is unavoidable. It is part of the process, and it is okay. From a physiological standpoint, anger increases your pulse and blood pressure. Adrenaline and Noradrenalin are the hormones that get elevated during anger. There are many

books and articles that deal with the nature of anger and how to manage it. Our course of action is to take anger and use it to our advantage.

Sometimes one stays in the anger stage for quite some time. It may take a while to figure out what your positive action will be. That's okay, because in the meantime, we can use the energy that comes from that anger. Some allow the anger to control them. They may go out and blow wads of money on clothes, cars or entertainment. They may use it as an excuse to be in a bad mood or unleash their emotions on some poor unwitting soul. But, let's be productive. If you feel angry, dig in your garden, clean your house, clean your car, clean your mother's house, and clean your friend's house. Clean your house again. When I was going through my divorce, my house was so clean. There was no clutter. Dust didn't even settle on my fake plants. But, you get my point. My mother polished the silver during my divorce, a chore usually delegated to my father the night before a grand dinner party. She could have spit nails she was so angry during the divorce period, but our family silver looked sparkling.

My mother was, in fact, the actual inventor of this next anger management tool. It is important to know my mother and I share similar interests in fashion, architecture, and home decorating. Because of these shared interests, we often share magazines. One day she handed me a magazine hoping it would get my mind off other matters. The magazine felt rather odd. It was light and the binding felt uneven. I must have looked puzzled, because she suddenly confessed that she had taken out the advertisements. I was still confused. Taking out the inserts and some pages of advertisements still did not account for the shape of the magazine. My mother explained she always took out the

little inserts; they drove her crazy and usually fell out anyway. She realized that still did not explain the newly acquired shape of the magazine. She went further to say "...well, I just took out the raunchier ads that are in magazines nowadays..." And then she giggled. She professed she had gotten so upset over the divorce proceedings the night before that she started ripping out every advertisement. She said it started out with a rip here and another rip a few pages later. She said the physical pulling and the auditory rip made her feel so much better. Besides, she was helping me get to the meat of the magazine much faster. She had found a coping skill to deal with anger. Go buy a magazine and start tearing.

Anger is an emotion that takes hold of not just your mind but also your body and spirit as well. It is good if you can find something physical with which to control and channel it. If you can find something you don't want to do, sometimes with anger as the driving force, you can get it accomplished in no time flat. Simple chores such as washing your car, washing your windows, dusting your furniture, re-organizing your underwear drawer or painting the powder room can be completed during this phase of anger. I painted my master bathroom three times. Sometimes just plain old exercise is beneficial.

When I was in my anger mode, I got a little defiant, too. I did some fun things just for me. I never did anything to harm anyone or hurt myself. Prior to my divorce my friends wanted me to clean the toilets with my ex-husband's toothbrush and not tell him. He can rest easy I did not. I chose to do things that lifted my spirit and not bring me down to a lower level of maturity. For example, my ex-husband did not like pink or frilly items or anything girly. And he definitely liked things his way. So, in my now new home, I

put pink hydrangeas in my living room…six to be exact. I put purple flowers on either side of my bed. I decorated my daughter's room in so much pink it looks like Pepto-Bismol exploded in the room. I even hung towels in the kitchen with pretty flowers and paisley designs. I went so far as to buy paper towels with flowers on them. I used to leave the bed unmade for days and would leave dishes in the sink overnight.

I would never do anything actually harmful but did things that did not really matter how one did them. I got pure joy out of leaving my son's toy trains out overnight or paying bills before the actual due date. I might have lost a few cents in interest paying bills extra early, but I found the reward worth it. Those dishes did find their way to the dishwasher and I did make my bed eventually, because I admit, I am a bit of a neat freak, too. But, it just gave me such a feeling of freedom and power. And, I knew I would not get verbally reprimanded for it later.

Many times we seek revenge when we are angry. I am human; I sought revenge, too. I work for a group of phenomenal Neurosurgeons who are fabulous. When I say fabulous, I mean more than just their work performance. Their attitude and personalities are incredible. Every so often they like me to tell the story of my revenge. Several of them have been divorced and know oh too well the perils of that road. I like to refer to my revenge story as my "Chocolate Moose Story," mainly because I like chocolate, and the story is about a moose. I start out by telling them what a wonderful hunter my ex-husband was and is. I always pipe in *"he spent enough time at it, he should be good."* They always get a kick out of that statement.

But seriously, he really is a talented hunter. He has hunted in Alaska, Oklahoma, Kansas, Colorado and who knows where else. Well, while we were married, he shot a beautiful moose. I always wanted to build a house and put the moose over a rock fireplace. Anyway, during our divorce proceedings, I petitioned to have the moose. I knew all along if I were awarded the moose, I would sell it, which would feel great. Well, I was awarded the moose. I held onto that moose for quite some time, and people got a kick out of the fact that it sat in my garage with a painter's tarp over it for a few years. Then I met a doctor (not in our group) who wanted the beast. He now has the moose hanging in his game room. He and his boys love it and at Christmas they decorate the moose all up, even with Christmas lights all over its antlers. The doctors I work with get such a kick out of the fact that I took the moose knowing I was never going to use it for its intended purpose and that they know the doctor who has it and exactly where the moose is to this day. Each of us enjoys the pictures of the moose all dolled up for the holidays.

As much as we want to constantly be doing something to get through this stage of anger, sometimes *time* is the healer. If you have children, this one is a little hard to swallow. I was given this piece of information when I divorced and did not want to believe it to be true. It is so true. I continue to tell my friends who get divorced about it. Sometimes it will take two years for your anger to dissolve. The reason for this is because it takes a full two years to go through an entire evolution of alternating holidays. One year, you have your children for Christmas and your ex has them the next; you have them for Thanksgiving, then your ex does; spring breaks, the 4th of July, and so on and so forth. It takes two years. But for some reason at the end of the two years, ya

kinda look at it and say, "yep this sucks, but this is my new normal."

During that time, you learn to take advantage of the time you don't have them on Christmas and get to shop the after-Christmas sales. You learn to do Thanksgiving early. That year your Thanksgiving Day off from work is a relaxing one and not a day of rushing from one family's house to another. You realize you can go to adult holiday parties without arranging for babysitting. And to be honest when you do have them on the actual holiday, it makes it that much more special to you. You really appreciate that time with them.

I have told my children it is not the life I wanted for them, but we must find the good. We have chosen to find the good in that they get to celebrate their birthdays twice. They get two days of Christmas. How exciting to be a child and experience your stocking and opening gifts twice. We have just made it part of our family motto to say, "we have to find the good." It has taught my children that no matter the circumstance, their parents' divorce, school situations or others, we must look for and seek the good. It may not be obvious or come to us immediately, but we search until we are able to make a bad situation at the very least tolerable. But sometimes, even that takes a little doing.

Anger can be an interesting emotion. My marriage counselor told me if I felt anger towards my husband, it meant the pendulum could swing back and I could love again. He went further to say that when you feel nothing is when it is all over. I felt nothing for years. This lack of emotion was reinforced upon the night I saw red. I began to see things from a different point of view. Then I tried hard to remain angry. I tried to summon up anger, but I had no emotion, just nothing…nothing. The counselor had been

right. I had immediate closure on the marriage. I knew it was finished. I just had to go through the steps of getting out of the relationship.

You may realize bitterness finds you. It may come when you think how you and your children were treated, lied to or neglected by the man you trusted and loved.
You may wonder how this could have happened from someone who was supposed to have been loving towards you. He had promised to honor and cherish you. Now your little girl fantasy has been shattered.

Here is the big message. You have to learn to accept the situation. I came to understand, I was not just angry with my ex-husband. I was angry with myself. I had to see those actions of his and mine as the past. I could not change what he or I had done. I had to forgive him and myself. It did not mean I had to continue to allow the behavior or stop the natural consequences as a result of that behavior from happening. I no longer had to be married. Here is a choice you can make. You can let your past haunt you or propel yourself forward. One way you can do this is by never allowing another human being to disrespect you like that again. When you are able to pull a positive action out of resentment and anger, you are ready to let go of the anger.

Work through your emotions, until you are ready to move on to your future. Talk it out. Remember "bitch'n" burns calories, too. Going through grief and anger is just part of the process. These emotions are another step to get you to your new life. Allow yourself the time to heal. Remember, there was preparation before running the half marathon. The training was hard. The race itself was hard. But the finish line is oh so sweet!

Chapter 7

MY TURN!

The room was brightly lit. I immediately noticed that the desks did not have the familiar brown rectangular tops with black metal legs. These desks were in the shape of a half squished octagon. The tops were colored in light blue and pale yellow. There were new unknown faces at each desk. My teacher's name was Ms. Costanza and in my eyes, she was the most beautiful third grade teacher at my new school. My family had just moved to Milan, Italy. At the time, my father worked for IBM and was transferred on assignment. My parents had enrolled me at the American School of Milan (ASM). It was I, me all by myself, standing just inside the doorway waiting to meet my new classmates. I was all alone. I don't remember every detail as to how I made friends, but I did it.

I soon was telling tales at the dinner table of who made "First Captain" and "Second Captain" on the playground. My brother would just roll his eyes at how stupid it all sounded, but it was serious business to my friends and me. It was how my group of friends kept up with who got to decide what we would play and how we would play each day on the playground. If you were mean or went against the First Captain, you were booted out of the circle of friends immediately. It would be up to the First Captain if you would be allowed back into the circle. To my recollection, the Second Captain had no real role unless for some reason the First Captain was sick or not at school that day. This safety net was activated from time to time.

VADEN INC.

But, I have regressed. Although my time in Italy was a good one that I look back on with fond memories, I think back on my first day at ASM and see in my mind's eye a scared but determined little girl. My personality and talents were all that I had to rely on that day. I used who I was to make friends. I found myself feeling much like that little girl standing in the doorway after my divorce. I felt alone and scared. Luckily for me, I had had that experience, even though long ago, to remind me I could make it. Just I, by myself, am an okay way to go. I had kept my little girl determination, and I was going to use all of it that I could muster to get through this divorce.

That being said I hope you will listen very carefully to this next part. At this moment you need to work on you before you can make it work with another person. I am fully aware that you may want to share your life with another or at the very least have someone to do adult activities with you. That in itself is a good thing. All I am saying is that it is important to find yourself, because you are important to get to know. You have more strength than you ever knew. You are a whole person by yourself. Right now you may feel insecure about yourself with whatever it is you are dealing with; that is normal. But you will grow into a confident human being if you search for who you are first and then search for someone to compliment your qualities and to work with your partner's strengths. Otherwise, you are just filling voids of loneliness.

I have heard it said, "You need to know what you are looking for." I say it is just as important to know what you don't want and won't put up with next time. You just got a first hand, front row seat to what you don't like. It took me the first three years of my marriage to figure out what I did not want

and the next seven to find the courage and strength to get out of the marriage. At this point when you see unwanted characteristics in others, high tail it out of there. Since you have been through or are going through a divorce, you are learning invaluable information. If you start dating again, you will have one up on your girlfriends who have never been married. You will be able to identify what you don't want; it will be easy to spot. If you can't see or figure out the patterns, seek professional help or ask a trusted friend.

Before you go and get all excited or worried about the dating process, let's find you. You are worth it. While you are dealing with your past and putting it in perspective, we can work on you. You must understand that you are bigger than this moment in time. Your lifespan will encompass thousands and thousands of moments. This divorce moment does not have to define who you are. You can use it as any other event in your life. Get through it and move on with the rest of your life.

Going through a divorce can cause you to lose a bit of yourself. You forget who you are. You can buy into the way the relationship made you feel unworthy. You can feel very bewildered at where you've come from and have no idea where you are headed. You can lose confidence in yourself. Basically, you can lose sight of who you are.

On the positive side, your divorce has given you some powerful information. You have learned what you don't like. Yep, it is just as important as knowing what you want. This is important so you can stop making the same choices that put you in this situation in the first place. You need to recognize those red flags and caution signs before you get hurt next time.

This means you get to be a little selfish for a moment in time. You have just separated or gotten a divorce and need to redefine who you are or who you want to be. In order for this to happen, you must get to know yourself again. When I got divorced, I had no idea how to accomplish this. Prior to my divorce, I remembered my marriage counselor giving me the assignment to go home and do something for myself. I could not think of anything to do. He had to break it down very simply for me. He told me to start out with taking a shower or a bubble bath. He then told me to try eating my favorite candy bar. This is when I discovered I could not tell you what my favorite anything was anymore. I had put all my likes and favorites on the back burner. My decision-making process had been stunted. I used to qualify everything against my husband's likes and dislikes.

I started by remembering my favorite color, as a child had been blue. I decided to choose a favorite flower, hydrangeas, which made it easy when decorating my living room. I kept asking myself questions. I discovered my three things I was willing to spend extra money on: cars, shoes and dark chocolate. The more I discovered about myself, the better equipped I felt to make decisions for myself. I remembered I loved to dance and started taking ballroom dancing lessons. I felt myself feeling very well grounded. I even realized people were interested in my thoughts and why I liked or disliked something. People began to respect my likes and dislikes. At work there is a bag of dark chocolate just for me even though most like the milk chocolate. Everyone knows I go to bed early but get up super early; no one calls me late, except for emergencies. I am still in the process of discovering me. But the journey is what has made it fun to explore new options. You don't have to be like everyone else. I have learned I am unique

and that is okay. Everyone else is unique and I respect that as well.

So, make a list of questions and answer them. What is your favorite color, wine, food, and dessert? Do you like the mountains or the beach? If you could be an animal, what would you choose and why? These are all types of questions we asked as a child to our friends, and we used to freely answer. We did not care if the answer changed in two days. My daughter's favorite color changes with her outfits she wears or is dependent on what her schoolteacher's favorite color is. Ask yourself what you want to be when you grow up. Sound silly? My Dad used to ask himself this often. He died at 73 years old, still saying he didn't know what he was going to do when he grew up.

Go to the library. Walk the aisles and read the titles of the books. See which ones draw you. Make note of the ones you actually pull off the shelf. Which ones do you check out? This is a good activity for you money pinchers (like me) out there. You can self-discover without spending a dime. If you see you enjoy surfing, great. But before you book a trip to the coast, purchase a wet suit, pay for the hotel and lessons, etc., you can read all about it. And then if the heat, sand and lack of coordination stop you, all you have to do is return the book. You have not lost anything. You have gained knowledge on a subject, you've made yourself a better-rounded person, and you've become a better conversationalist. You don't even have to go to the library in this day and age. You can just surf the Internet for things that may interest you.

Another good way to get to re-know you is through your parents. I am sure they are all too well aware of who you are. I bet they could dredge up some good stories. You

could ask some old school mates or family friends. You know the ones. The friends who have been around so long they seem like family; you may even call them Uncle Tom or Aunt Josie. These are powerful people to you right now.

I admit when I did this exercise I was concerned, I am not much of an extrovert anyway and the last thing I wanted to do was share my problems. I thought people would think less of me or feel sorry for me for going through a divorce. I was wrong. I enjoyed myself immensely, and it reminded me of whom I had been and helped me get back to my old disposition that I had lost. The great thing was, now I got to add my confidence and strength to my old characteristics. I am the new and improved model of me.

So, keep a running list of your qualities. When you run into a snag or if you currently struggle, whip out your list and see what you can draw on to help you cope.

A "Georgia Peach" is what I claim to be. I was born in New Orleans where my father used to tell me I was "The Queen of New Orleans where they eat those rice and beans." I heard that all my life. But after my father had a three-year assignment in Milan, Italy, we moved and stayed in Atlanta until I went to college. Any way you throw the dice, I am a southern bell. My southern accent comes out when I get tired or I am around my Southern friends for an extended period of time.

I took a trip with my children back to Atlanta when I was getting my divorce. I reunited with old family friends and even some old high school friends. As mentioned earlier, I was a little concerned to do this at first. I thought people would think less of me or worse, feel sorry for me since I was going through a divorce. Once I started visiting, I

enjoyed myself so much, and it reminded me of who I had been and helped me get back to my old disposition.

Further, it reminded me of those in my past who believed in me. It reminded me of the compliments and good things people had said about me. Visiting with those who have known you for years can be inspirational. It can be like hearing a good reference about you. Most referrals ask that you have known the person for at least two or three years. The reason is because that means you really know the person. If you are unable to travel, at least think of those compliments you have gotten in your past.

While in Atlanta I had dinner with a very close family friend. After dinner while the children were playing quietly, we gathered in her living room. She had recently found some of her ancestors' love letters. She began to read the letters out loud in chronological order. I was mesmerized. I was caught up in the love story of two people who had lived just moments before my lifetime. I did not want the evening to end. Well, my friend immersed herself into a project of compiling those love letters and even publishing them.

Her book reminds me now that sometimes love needs a bigger audience, and I am proud of her accomplishment. At the time, I remember thinking there was hope for love. My marriage had just ended, but that did not mean I would never love again. I had a lot of love to give. I knew I would heal and recover from divorce.

I was once privy to a conversation a group of ladies at a restaurant were having. To be perfectly honest, I was only privy because I was actually eavesdropping. But, what I overheard was intriguing. It did not matter what their discussion was about; shopping, movies, vacations, their

husbands (I assumed). Their opinions were flying. One lady would say she loved to shop at Neiman's, another would say she found the best buys at Nordstrom's. Yet another lady would tell of the shoe department available at another store. I think they all agreed that the movie that was out at the time was really good. I started to wonder if they were even hearing each other at all. Maybe they were just wrapped up in their own words. You know the kind. Some people like to talk just to hear their own voices. They don't have any actual advice or really anything to say. But then I decided it was a great idea... just talk.

It would be like trying on clothes to see if they fit, but in this scenario, trying on ideas to see if you agree or not. Try it some time. Get a bunch of your friends together and start asking questions. (Do not tell them why you're doing this.) You could get the ball rolling by asking about the latest movie or new restaurant that just opened. See if anyone saw it, or liked it. Then just keep asking different questions. You will learn about yourself. It is hard to resist putting your thoughts out there when everyone is sharing theirs. When you are in the comfort of friends it makes it easier to be more open as well. I learned quite a bit about those ladies that day. Just start talking; you may learn something about yourself.

After divorce, your life begins in a new awkward and stilted manner. Your life is forever changed. The process of dealing with that new life and going about your daily business without that person is daunting. Eventually, your new life will take precedence over the old. Your mind will stop thinking of your current problems and old way of life. This doesn't mean you won't remember or certain things won't trigger your memories. Think of it this way. When you were in high school the events that took place probably felt

so important at the time. Who was dating who, who was taking so and so to the dance, what dress was she going to wear? Whose parents bought whom a car? How many of us heard something like, "my parents are just going to kill me!" "I failed my math test."

This scenario really did happen to me. I was in sixth grade. I had just been handed my math test back with an "F". I can remember being totally stressed out as I told my friend how one of my father's majors in college had been math. For heaven's sake, he was an Engineer from Georgia Tech, and I knew he was GOING TO KILL ME. To this day I can remember how the sunlight shone through the trees and thinking that would be the last daylight I would ever enjoy. To my astonishment my father told me to just do better next time, because in 20 some odd years no one would know or care. He was right. No one on a job interview has ever asked me about that blasted test. And, I now work for brain surgeons, so I must not be too inept a person. I tell you this to explain my point. Today your crisis is important, but with time, the emotion will not be as strong as it is today. I still remember that test and how I felt. It is just not as raw a feeling today. Time is a healing factor; it takes time to focus on new "normal" things. Cut yourself some slack.

But this is the time in your life you can make it all about you. And…it is okay. What have you done for yourself lately? This is a tough one and I still struggle with it. I am sure most, if not all, moms and people pleasers such as I can relate to my resistance to this method. You must be good to yourself and take care of your body and soul.

To this day, when I spend money on myself I get close to a panic attack. I don't know why, I have the money and I have a good job. I think I am just more comfortable in the role of

the giver. Also, if I am being totally honest, I have to remind myself that I *am* worth it. Many women get a charge out of shopping…I do not. I will never forget the day I went shopping with one of my nearest and dearest friends. I had allotted myself $1,500 to spend and had told my friend so. We shopped and shopped, she made me try on I don't know how many outfits. And yes, I did say, "made" me, because I do not have shopping stamina.

Well, at the end of our adventure, I had spent a little over $1,000. Now mind you, I had not spent anywhere near my designated amount. But, I thought I was going to pass out. Seriously, I became short of breath, I had to splash cold water on my face; I even had to find a place to just sit for a minute. My friend laughed at me the entire time. She kept logically telling me that I had not even spent what I had set aside to spend, and the last time I had bought anything for myself had been over seven months ago. (Only a best friend would have those numbers down and ready to use against you.)

But, none of that changed how I was feeling. And then she looked me right in the eyes and said "You know you're worth it, right?" She went on, "Tell me, you know you are worth it." She had me; she had gone straight to the root of the problem. But just identifying the problem was not good enough for her. Our friendship is too strong. We each know how the other ticks and what it takes to make a change. And that's when she used it against me to her advantage. So she went on…"You buy new clothes for your son and daughter, and you get great pleasure out of that." "But they need to see you get new clothes and see you get pleasure, so you will teach them to care for themselves and they will know they are worth it." Enough said; I got it.

My children are my heart, and I want to raise them to be healthy productive adults. Learning to take care of yourself is important for your well-being. But, it also teaches those around you your self-worth and how you should be treated as well. So, take a moment to be good to yourself. It may be as small a gesture as taking a bubble bath, picking out your favorite candy bar, folding your bathroom towels just the way you like. Whatever you can think of, pamper yourself each day, even in the smallest ways.

If you have taken the time to get to know yourself again and you feel comfortable, you could start thinking about the type of partner you would like this next go-round. The more you know about yourself, the more equipped you are at figuring out what you want on your next love adventure. Remember you are smarter than you were before, so arm yourself with all your knowledge when seeking this person. Before getting into another relationship write down the characteristics you want and now know you will not put up with in your future mate. Do not just put it in your mind. Put it on paper. This will assure you, you will not be skewed by the person you start to date. You will forget everything on your list when the butterflies start floating. And all those characteristics you do not want will seem acceptable; you might even try to settle.

I feel that I was not part of a good marriage, so I have upgraded in my life. My life at this point is wonderful. Why would I want to make another poor decision to go back into another bad marriage? Being lonely is not a good enough driving force; I was lonely in my marriage and being lonely now is not a new emotion. You want to be able to make a sound decision with your mind and not just let the butterflies in your stomach make the choice. Use all your resources next time around, including what you have learned from your previous broken relationship.

You may still be wondering if you should date or not. Yikes, that is a good one. Here is some sound advice I was given. Start by feeling comfortable with the opposite sex just as friends. See how these friends treat you and let that be the standard against which you judge possible partners. Let your friends teach you the respect you deserve, also, the quality of person of which you now demand and seek.

One of my closest friends is a man. He takes me out and wines and dines me. He treats me like a princess. And yet, we are just friends. However, this relationship has become extremely important in my decision-making. If I go out on a date now, how that man treats me is compared to how my friend treats me. I have gotten rid of some poor quality men, real quickly, just by knowing how I can and deserve to be treated. I do not even have to waste my time trying to figure it out or wonder if we were together, if he might treat me differently. It is black and white and so easy to see.

Since I had been off the dating market a while I had to get up to speed, so I thought. There seemed to be a new dating language, a new way to find people to date. In came Internet dating. Everyone has advice for you on this subject, not every piece of advice is good or makes sense. Some of the new rules presented to me were things like he must call on Wednesday for a date on Friday. He can call on Thursday for a Saturday date. You must never accept if he calls for the next night and, you must be busy if he calls to take you out for the same day that he is calling. My head was already spinning. I was not sure I understood the first rules.

My single friends kept going with these new laws of dating land. Never discuss where you are in your relationship or

define how serious you are within the relationship. If you do, he must bring it up first. The list went on and on. I found the rules to be silly and high-schoolish. I did not understand Internet dating. I questioned why it was considered taboo to put a singles ad in the newspaper, but all of a sudden it was okay to place it with a singles Internet site. And to go further, why couldn't people lie on the dating service anymore than they would in the newspaper? I must admit some of my friends that followed these rules are currently married.

I say, and this truly is my opinion, I am a mother and a woman in my thirties, soon to be forties. I only date men who are self-assured, well established in their professions, polite to all, including the wait staff, but who don't flirt with every creature in a skirt, are respectful of my time and position in life. I don't waste my time on the others. I have much more important things to do with my life. But the choice is yours. If you want to sift through the masses and have the time and energy to do so, be my guest.

As for me, I decided to move slowly through those dating waters. I have a serious job and am thrilled with being a mother. I enjoy being selfish with my time and not having to make any excuses to spend every moment that I can with my children. I know there will come a point in my life or the right man will come along, when I know I will be ready.

Maybe right now you're not ready. Maybe you're not sure you want to date yet. Or maybe you want to try your newfound self on for size first. If this is the case have a crush. A crush keeps you looking good. If you think you may see this person, you start to dress nicer and take better care of yourself.

Having a crush can be fun. Search for someone who is real. Don't make them up in your head. Find someone you know or know of at least. They must be real, because you must be able to see them for who they are, flaws and all. A celebrity is always a safe bet. You know you won't really see these people, but it's just amusing. Tell only those close to you, so no one will think you are crazy or an actual stalker.

My crush was on movie star Owen Wilson. At that time, I needed humor in my life more than ever. I thought he was hilarious. Besides his being funny, I was drawn to the cadence of his voice. I found it very attractive and soothing. I rented any Owen Wilson movie I could get my hands on. I would put the children to bed and then play his movies over and over again. I would rent them and return them at the very last minute to squeeze out every moment. I finally became embarrassed enough renting the same movies over and over, that I went ahead and bought one. I should have thought of that sooner. But when you're going through a divorce you're not always working on all cylinders. The movie "Cars" came out about that same time. I'm not sure if my children or I were more excited to see the movie. For them it was the obvious animation, but for me, Owen Wilson had a voiceover in it. I just listened to his voice. It was the best children's movie I ever heard.

My cousin, which whom I am very close, knew of my Owen Wilson crush. She played right along. She would hear of or see on TV where or what he had been doing. She would call me and say things like, "the media is showing Owen in New York this weekend, I thought he was at your house." And then she would just laugh. Playing right along, I would shoot back with some answer like "yeah, I know, he is here, he just put a decoy out so the press would leave him alone

with me." It became more difficult when he got girlfriends, but we would just pretend the media had played that up for his movie premiere. All innocent, and rest assured, Mr. Wilson does not have a stalker.

To tie this all together, I would make remarks about things I had learned about myself. For example, I would tell my cousin we were going to the beach, because he knew that was my favorite vacation spot. Or we went out to dinner last weekend, and he opened the car door for me. Silly little things just to try them on for size. I put them out there in the universe. And we got a little amusement out of it, too. As you can see, my gift of creativity can get a bit deranged, but it worked at the time. You might find a little craziness does you some good, too.

Chapter 8

QUOTES:

If I had a nickel for every time I heard someone say...

A white marble box sits on my vanity in my bathroom. It is a 5x5 inch square container with a flat marble lid that rests on top with an inscription. The words read "NEVER, NEVER, NEVER Give up." This is my most beloved quote. Winston Churchill said this in a speech to the English people during World War II. Persistence is the name of the game. Days will be hard during and after your divorce. There will be days you won't feel strong. There will be days you think all hope is lost. Keep on anyway. Hopefully, you have built a team of people to surround you and help you during your darkest moments. But if you have no one, and I believe there are some who have no safety net or any support, use this book to find your way to gain the strength and power to do it yourself. Be your own best friend. Then turn around and help someone just like you. I know for myself, if I'm going down, I'm going down with a fight. I don't know how to give up or give in. I read this quote every morning. I have found that quotes and the written word can be very powerful.

The first year I went to college my parents settled me into my dorm room and went to Europe on a six-week vacation. Right before they left me, my mother became very sentimental and wrote me a letter. It was a sweet letter from

a good mother to her daughter. In the letter she had handwritten a scripture that talks about God's love and how we can never be separated from Him and His love. She then added at the bottom of the note, even though she would be far away, nothing could separate our love from each other. Ever since then, she and I have handwritten or typed out scriptures for each other. We have found that seeing the scripture in a cursive or a beautifully typed computer font can make the passage come alive. It can seem that the words just jump right off the page. This can be done with other quotes, passages or inspirational words. If you like to needlepoint or cross-stitch you might enjoy putting an inspirational passage on fabric and making a pillow out of it. If you like to paint, you could cover an entire wall with your favorite phrases. You could just write out the words and frame them and then hang them in a frequented area of your home. Then words of encouragement would be all around to comfort and support you.

While going through my divorce, little phrases or golden nuggets as I call them would get said. I started to write them down, so I could refer back to them. I have compiled a few of my favorites that really struck a chord with me. I have become a fond gatherer of quotes.

If I misquote Ivana Trump, I sincerely apologize for it right now. I have given her credit for this saying every time I have used it. One evening I was watching a biography on Ivana Trump. During one of the interviews she was discussing her life path after divorce from Donald Trump. During the course of this interview, I learned one, how she manages to maintain her figure. She explained that once she arrives at her destination she orders a dozen boiled eggs from the hotel kitchen and keeps them in the room's refrigerator. Seeing that she was an out-of-the-box thinker I immediately,

in my mind, declared her credible. This woman had me hooked as she talked about her business endeavors and life after divorce. But it wasn't until the interviewer tried to get her to say something spiteful against Donald Trump that I became an Ivana Trump fan. She looked at the interviewer like she didn't even know who he was talking about and replied "Looking good is the best revenge." I laughed out loud, but I took it to heart. I get pure joy on those days that I get all dressed up and people say, "What was your ex-thinking?" I just grin and then they add, "He obviously wasn't." That's when I give Ivana Trump a mini high five in my mind.

Humor is one of the ways I handle life. I cannot shut that side of my brain off to save my life. For some reason, my mind is constantly finding the absurdity in any given situation. My friends tell me it is my quick wit and dry since of humor that gets me into trouble. Ironically, I consider myself a very serious person. However, humor for me breaks up the tension and stress that builds in a room or around a problem. One of my dearest of friends knows this about me. What makes it fun is that he is highly intelligent, and it makes banter back and forth a great thrill to try and one up the other.

During one of our "serious" discussions one day, he made a humorous comment that I told him had to go in my book. He told me to think of my divorce like an easy diet...he sheepishly said, "You just lost about a hundred and ninety-five pounds of yourself that you didn't like. And the best part, you will never gain him back again."

Lisa Gastineau is another woman I like to quote. She was married to Mark Gastineau a football player for the Jets. Later they divorced. And she had a television reality show

with her daughter. On one of the episodes an interviewer asked her who she was dating, any man in particular right now? Her response was what was so funny. She replied… "Nope, no <u>man</u> in particular, every woman needs nine or ten of them." That's always made me sniggle a bit.

A little more cerebral thinking, Albert Einstein once said, "The definition of insanity is continuing to do the same thing over and over again, expecting a different outcome." There came a point in my marriage where I felt I had tried to do everything I could to save the marriage. I even started doing the same things over again, thinking maybe they would be different this time. But then I was reminded of this quote.

Remind yourself for now or in future relationships Albert Einstein's definition of insanity. Try something new if what you are doing is not working. Do you notice you keep getting the same kind of men in your life? Maybe you are doing something to attract that type of man. Or maybe for some reason you are attracted to a personality type. Figure out what it is and why and just stop; stop the insanity. Take control of your actions.

An old college acquaintance of mine told me he was getting ready to have his second divorce. I looked at him in shock and wonder. He forthrightly told me he kept choosing the same type of woman. He proceeded to add he knew he needed to change. Don't keep making the same mistake over and over again. It's insane.

Remember you don't have to make big elaborate plans for tomorrow when going through your divorce. Sometimes just getting out of bed is your achievement for the day. Be proud of yourself for the small efforts you make, they will eventually add up and make a big difference.

A brown wooden podium resides in my Sunday school classroom. On the front is a brass plaque with an inscription. The message reads "Always fight with the sun at your back." This podium belongs to a man for whom I have profound respect. His wife gave it to him as a gift. He stands behind it each week as we go through class.

As the seasons pass and time rolls on, I can see in my mind's eye, fathers telling sons this piece of advice. "Son, always fight with the sun at your back." I have found this quote to be very refreshing. Sometimes the simplest of ideas can make the biggest impact on our outcomes.

The following are more quotes to which I often refer. No explanation is really needed. I remember having a very short attention span when I was going through my divorce. I wished then that I could find something to read quickly to give me encouragement and strength. Maybe one of the following will provide just that in your life. If not, listen to those around you; sometimes people say the most profound things. The Internet is also a great resource. And of course, it's a great "mind trick". See if you can find a golden nugget to grasp onto.

Teresa Avery, RNfa
"Divorce is a sacrifice for your children"

Teresa Avery, RNfa
"Divorce can be a test of perseverance in integrity"

Susan Butcher, Iditarod Winner 1988
"I do not know the word 'quit'. Either I never did, or I have abolished it.

Mac Jemison, NASA Astronaut
"Never limit yourself because of others' limited imagination; never limit others because of your own limited imagination."

Mother Theresa, Social Activist
"I know God will not give me anything I can't handle. I just wish that He didn't trust me so much."

Stephen Kaggwa
"Try and fail, but don't fail to try."

Robert H. Schuller
"Failure doesn't mean you are a failure it just means you haven't succeeded yet."

Thomas Edison
"Many of life's failures are people who did not realize how close they were to success when they gave up."

Sam Walton
"I had to pick myself up and get on with it, do it all over again, only even better this time."

Dan Custer
"Every morning is a fresh beginning. Every day is the world made new. Today is a new day. Today is my world made new. I have lived all my life up to this moment, to come to this day. This moment—this day—is as good as any moment in all eternity. I shall make of this day—each

moment of this day—a heaven on earth. This is my day of opportunity."

Jewish Proverb
God is closest to those with broken hearts

Alexander Graham Bell
"When one door closes, another opens; but we often look so long and so regretfully upon the closed door that we do not see the one which has opened for us."

Lisa Marie Williams
"Only you can control your future and you need to start making choices that will eventually bring you to your new life."

Dove Chocolate wrapper
"Try something new today."

Vince Lombardi
"It's not whether you get knocked down; it's whether you get up."

Unknown
"Anyone can hold the helm when the sea is calm."

Dale Carnegie
"Most of the important things in the world have been accomplished by people who have kept on trying when there seemed to be no hope at all."

Unknown
"People do what they want to do."

Unknown
"The best predictor of future behavior is past behavior."

Hebrew Talmud (sayings and teachings of Rabbis)
"Be very careful if you make a woman cry, because God counts her tears. The woman came out of a man's rib. Not from his feet to be walked on. Not from his head to be superior, but from the side to be equal. Under the arm to be protected and next to the heart to be loved."

Albert Einstein
"Insanity is doing the same thing over and over again, but expecting different results."

Albert Einstein
"It's not that I'm that smart, it's just that I stick with problems longer."

Chapter 9

MONEY!

"Money, Money, Always sunny, in a rich man's world" ABBA

The room was a landmine of stashed dollar bills and coins. It did not matter what time of year it was, I always had a little stash of cash. My brother on the other hand, spent his money the moment he got it. One time he approached me with an offer. He wanted me to help him save his money. He wanted me to act like a bank. He even went so far as to attach interest each month if he did not withdraw his money from my room/bank. I was excited at the idea of setting up a bank. I started thinking of names for my bank. Also, I thought I would need to create little deposit slips. As I started to think about how I could use rubber stamps to keep everything organized, I wondered where the money would come from for the monthly interest. My brother explained I had enough money saved to make up that difference. That did not sit quite right with me, so I took counsel with my advisors, also known as Mom and Dad. This scheme did not sit well with them either, and the whole thing went bust. My brother continued to spend like mad, and I continued to gather and save. It became second nature. My saving pattern continued into my adult life and kicked into overdrive after my divorce.

My lawyer could hardly contain herself, all she could get out was "You have a problem." With tears of laughter rolling

down her face and gasping for air she kept blurting out..."You have a problem." I just sat there waiting for the explanation, I didn't think I had a problem; I thought I was being smart. She would compose herself and ask another question. I would seriously answer her. Again, the laughter came. Finally, she was able to speak. She told me, I had the opposite problem that most people have. She said she usually has to have a serious talk with her clients on how to stop spending money. But with me, she had to tell me how to *spend* money.

This was not news to me. I have always saved money. I used to keep the actual coins my grandfather gave me, just because he had touched them. It was sentimental that he gave me something. As well, my friends try to get me to spend money, too. But, more than my spending habits, she was astonished at the amount of money I had saved just four years after from my divorce. The only debt I had was my mortgage and car payment; at any time I could have paid off my car and still had enough in the bank. Not to mention my hiding places where I stashed actual cash in case something went dreadfully wrong with the banks, the world or society as a whole.

I've come along way since then. I have come to understand the difference between living in scarcity and living in abundance. I used to scrape and save every dollar, and hide it away. I have done that since I was a little girl and had always had money. I did not understand at that point the principles of creating wealth. I learned to use money to my advantage.

One of the first things I realized about money is that it holds power. When I was newly divorced, I did two things that have been my driving force to get and keep me financially

independent. The first was to learn exactly what it took to maintain my household on the bare minimum. I made a list of all my expenditures and what it cost exactly. Anything that I saw as frivolous got cut immediately from my "just survive budget." I cut the Internet. At that time, I never used it at home and had access at work or knew I could use the libraries. I cut out hair appointments and manicures. One of my nurses at work used to cut my hair between patients for free. I cut my nails off short like the models in the magazines. Speaking of magazines, I dropped all my subscriptions knowing I could read them at the library for free. Since there was no need for a landline for most calls, I changed my phone landline to a limited plan. My work paid for my cell phone. I whittled and whittled at my budget until I was at the least amount that I could spend.

Then I averaged my monthly cost and multiplied that by twelve. I then knew what it would cost me to live for one year. That created my first goal, to save enough money in the bank to cover me for three months of living expenses. I figured if for some reason I lost my job, at the most, it would take me three months to find another. When I hit three months, the goal went up to six months. Once I had six months of living expenses covered, I started adding back a few other expenses. However, I kept a tight reign on it. I did not add the Internet back until just a few years ago and still wonder if my use of it justifies the monthly cost.

It became a game to see how much I could save. I would consider all my options before making any purchase. For example, when I get a hair cut now, I skip the blow dry and style. I buy generic brands when possible. I buy the children clothes from a gently used store. I found that Target makes durable inexpensive children's clothing, too, instead of paying department store pricing. I continued to

save until I had a year's worth of living expenses saved in the bank. Then I knew I had the power. I knew if something broke, something had to be replaced, if any kind of emergency arose, I was ready. I felt stable and in control. Then, in theory, anything over that year's expense mark has been mine for fun. I say in theory because I knew in the back of my head I would continue to save more.

The other thing I did when I got divorced was pretending I was a millionaire. I put my imaginary million dollars in my imaginary bank. Then I figured the amount of interest I could make from the money and subtracted my year's worth of expenses. I then had the amount leftover that I could in my imagination spend however I saw fit. What was interesting to me was there was not that much more I truly wanted to spend anywhere else. I thought about a trainer, a cook, a maid, a new wardrobe and, of course, new shoes. But with my newfound "savings game," I decided I could figure out how to better lift weights without a trainer. My children were young enough not to like fancy meals; I could still cook our basic dinners. A maid would be nice, but being a neat freak, I would probably clean before she got there. And as far as a new wardrobe and shoes, I was obtaining those with my current lifestyle. Maybe not all at once, but that was okay with me.

So, I realized, I was already living my millionaire lifestyle. No, I did not have four cars or houses on both coasts; I wasn't jetting off to Paris for the weekend. But my world was just fine. I am a money saver at heart, so it makes it easier for me. I continue to save and find ways to do things for less. It truly was like a game to me.

Watching your money grow can be fun. You don't have to be as extreme as I was. You can set up a new savings

account or just get a jar and fill it up with loose change. Think about what you might buy with your saved money. A new pair of shoes is always my favorite. Or maybe you want to save for a vacation. If you have children, you can involve them in the project. Having a family goal can help unite you as a family.

Just remember money is a resource. My father used to propose that if all the money in the world was gathered up and dispersed equally to every individual, it would take less than three years for the same people who have all the money now to have it again. That tells me that people are using something other than money to make it in life. They are using their education, intuition, drive, worldly instincts, natural talents and abilities to succeed. Our ability to survive is dependent on our use of all our resources, not just our money.

When dealing with money, there are a few practical matters that must be taken care of now that you are divorced. You may not want to think about death, but it is a part of life. What will happen to all your material items and possessions if you die? If you have children, how will they be protected and be able to benefit from what you have left them in this world? You need to create a will or change your will if you already have one in place. You need to change the beneficiaries on your stocks, life insurance policies, house mortgages, etc. I was fortunate to have a father who taught me so much about stocks, savings and how money works.

Surround yourself with success. This is the old "fake it 'til you make it" motto. Dress the part. Be around people you respect who are successful. The more you are around them the more you will see how they do things and react to things. You can then begin to mimic those ways in your own life.

You can learn to develop those habits that make them successful. My thought is to feel what it is like so much that you could even taste it and therefore become it and live it. The only word of caution is to remember your definition of success may be different from everyone else's. Be sure to clarify from the beginning what your goals and aspirations are.

My divorce lawyer told me I had many resources at my fingertips. She said I was in a very good position to help myself. She further explained she had seen and helped so many who had nothing after a divorce. I understood I had family, I had my education, and I had some money in the bank. However, I was angry with the judge. She had given my ex-husband our up- and-running business and assets to continue to create cash flow. My part of the settlement was stashed in my retirement fund. It had been rolled into an IRA fund. I thought if I could make it to retirement age, I would be a millionaire. I was living in the buy-and-hold theory. My father had set me up with an IRA since I had been in my teens. At that time, he told me to forget about the money, just pretend it never existed. He had told me most people run into trouble when they take the money out to buy a car and never put it back into the fund.

For years I had been of the mindset that the money really wasn't there. So, when I had been given money in the form of securities I thought, gee, thanks, that money didn't really exist. My lawyer told me to take the money and use it. I looked at her like she had lost her mind. I was living in scarcity. I did not understand how to use that money to propel myself forward.

I learned the world of using money to create wealth. I had to understand that I was not in competition with everyone else.

I had to learn how to put my money in the universe so it would come back to me with more money attached to it. I had to see I could create wealth in partnership and alongside of others. I had to live in abundance. I had to change my mindset. Once again, I gathered information and learned all that I could about money and our society today. The more knowledge I had, the more courage I had to try it. I kept educating myself until I was ready to put it into practice.

I lived in both worlds simultaneously for some time, one of scarcity and one of abundance. I wanted to let go completely. With every baby step that I made I would get a taste of the abundant life. Every step made me want more. It was exhilarating, exciting and most of all freeing. I found more control of my money and my life. Instead of waiting for the money to accumulate, I started living the life I had designed in my head.

You see the biggest barrier between you and your financial success is your mindset. After my divorce, I was living a mindset of scarcity. I had to change my mindset to abundance and prosperity. I now have and follow strategies to give me financial security.

You may think since you are not a millionaire you do not have much to keep organized. You need to keep what you have organized. They do not teach this in college. You need a will, disability insurance and accountants. Learn about trusts, estate planning, or opportunities to buy businesses to create cash flow. And this is at the bare minimum.

Finances are just another piece to regain control of your life. Your money is one of the strongest ways to rebuild your

foundation. Once I understood this new mindset of money, I knew I had to help and share this message with other women, specifically. It's not that it won't work for men (because it can and has), but I have a soft spot in my heart for women who have been through a divorce and choose to believe in themselves. I want to help those women excel. I am one of those women.

I understand today you either choose to live in scarcity or you choose abundance. Scarcity says there are limited resources, and I must live in competition with everyone else for those resources. Scarcity says I must collect and keep my money away from society. If I do not hold onto my money, someone might take my money and keep it. On the other hand, abundance says there is enough for everyone. Abundance says you don't have to be in competition with others but cooperate to help each other. It falls quite well into line with my Christian thoughts and behaviors. The Golden Rule for example. "Do unto others as you would have done unto you." It takes it another step further. Abundance is thinking creatively. It is learning to think outside of the box. It is viewing problems not as dead ends or obstacles, but as challenges. It is like divorce not being the end, but the beginning of something new.

As you know having a fondness for quotes, I like this one about the difference between scarcity and abundance.

"People with a scarcity mentality tend to see everything in terms of win-lose. There is only so much; and if someone else has it, that means there will be less for me. The more Principle-centered we become, the more we develop an abundance mentality, the more we are genuinely happy for the successes, well-being, achievements, recognition, and

good fortune of other people. We believe their success add to… rather than detracts from…our lives."

Stephen R. Covey

Scarcity shows us limits and ceilings. Abundance is boundless. There are no limits on creativity, ingenuity, innovation or invention. Our country continues to grow and remain strong under the principle of abundance. We have grown from the steam engine to jet fuel. And now, we stand at a moment in time where maybe an engine will be invented that does not demand oil. Oil in our times, may be thought of as a "limited resource." But those living in abundance see "limited" oil as an opportunity. It is these people with such vision that sent us to the moon, entertained us with the first music video and created the Internet. You educate, create, build and help others. You have a mind use it. And, do not be afraid to fail.

Thomas Edison failed thousands of times before creating the incandescent light bulb. He never gave up on the idea. Meanwhile, on the journey of failing all of those times, he patented electricity, batteries, cement, motion pictures, telegraphs, the telephone and others. He kept trying. It is interesting to me all the things he tried to use to make the incandescent light bulb. He tried carbon, boron, chromium, molybdenum (which I can't even pronounce), tungsten and nickel. He even tried platinum twice. The lesson is he kept trying. This reminds me of the quote from Albert Einstein, "It's not that I'm so smart, it's just that I stay with problems longer."

 It is up to you to determine how much money you feel comfortable with in the bank. How will you feel if the car breaks down, the dishwasher floods the house and the dryer

breaks down all at once? Another way to figure it is if you were to lose your job, how long do you think it would take you to find another one? You can only measure your level of security.

Once you have figured out your monthly cost of living, you can dream. Make your millionaire budget. Be honest with yourself. What would you put your money into if you were a millionaire? Would you like a weekly maid or a daily cook? Would you like to have a pool or become a member of a country club? Would you like to have several automobiles or would you like to be able to travel to exotic foreign lands? Would you like to go to New York for Fashion Week or would you like a new wardrobe each season? What do you deem important?

Chapter 10

Conclusion

Cleopatra, Queen Elizabeth of England, Bathsheba, Jezebel, Eve, and Joan of Arc - what other women come to mind from the past? Why do we know these women? Did they make a positive or a negative impact on the world in which they lived? When we look back in time, it is easy to think that these icons, whether good or bad, were the only ones who existed. Instead, there had to be so many more people who lived. Not everyone lived in castles or had beautiful gardens. If there was the rich and powerful, there must also have been the poor and weak to offset the two lifestyles.

When I think of women in the generations who have lived before, I wonder what influence if any I am leaving. I think about Bible characters. There had to be so many more people who lived who just didn't make the cut to be discussed in the Bible. I wonder if I had made it into the Bible, would God have used my life story as a "how to" example or a "beware of this way of life" story? What about all those people who didn't get written about specifically? Odds are I would be one of those.

Does basic human nature change? I believe human beings have been acting and struggling with the same principles and ideas since the beginning of our time. Our ability to survive is dependent on our use of our resources. You may have all the education a school can provide, a bank account

with unlimited funds, you may even have the power over other people's lives in business or countries, but you could lose it all. You must know how to manage what you have.

The History Channel is one of my favorite channels on television. I get made fun of for watching it and DVR'ing shows I want to watch later. I have found it fascinating to see how people of the ancient worlds dealt with life. It is intriguing to see how they would attack a problem with limited resources and far less knowledge of how the earth works than we have today. I have often wondered what great conquerors and kings would think about during the day. For example, what was Alexander the Great's first waking thought? I'm sure it wasn't to take a shower, walk the dog, have some breakfast or head off to the office in the Bentley. He must have been strategizing in his mind all the time.

I think it must have been hard in those times to learn to kill with a sword, or know barbarians could ravage your village, rape the women, take the children into slavery and burn the entire place to the ground. The fear of not having a harvest would take its toll on the mind. What about winter months with animal skins and fire to keep you warm? What about getting sick or needing surgery?

It was about survival then, and it is still about survival now. We still don't have all the answers. Our surroundings have changed, but it's still about surviving. Evolution hasn't stopped; you're just a part of it now. Time can move so slowly that we don't see the changes made in a lifetime.

My grandmother was shy of 102 years when she died. In her lifetime, she saw the invention of things like the car and the accomplishment of someone landing on the moon (which

she thought was a Hollywood production even though her son, my father, worked as an engineer on the space endeavors). She even saw the invention of pantyhose, which she always told me she could have done without.

The point is we must learn to survive with the resources that are available to us today. Sometimes it takes a little creativity and thinking outside the box. Maybe someday people will be talking about you in the history books, and be amazed at how you conquered this life the best you knew how.

This is now your life you decide what is important. Put your big girl panties on, put one flower foot in front of the other and go survive. Life is a journey, and we learn (hopefully) along the way.

I have come to learn that even though the world would like us to think life is about butterfly love, money and winning, it just is not. I'm here to tell you it is about surviving. Some would like to compare it to playing a game, but you can't. There are no timeouts, no half times, there's no asking the coach to put you on the bench for a while. It is much more simple…it's just about surviving. Look back over the centuries. People have been trying for years. Every day humans have been waking up fighting in wars, fighting the elements, fighting disease, fighting hunger, just fighting. At the root of it all is survival. But that does not mean you cannot survive and <u>flourish</u>! So, put on your heels and go out and fight the dragons.

Notes:

Notes:

15361456R00063

Made in the USA
Charleston, SC
30 October 2012